Of Malet, Malbis and Fairfax

A History of Acaster Malbis

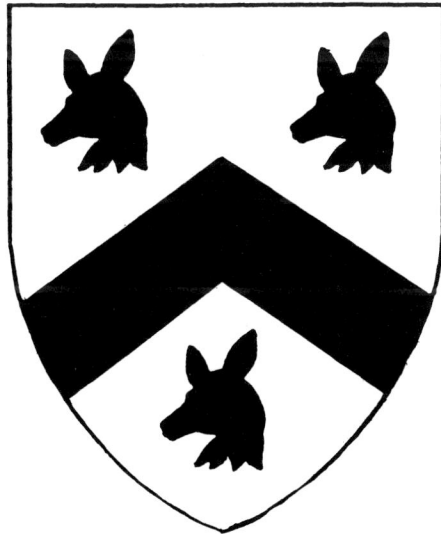

Acaster Malbis Millennium Book Group

C A Appleby and D B Smith (eds)

First published in 2000 by Acaster Malbis Millennium Book Group
c/o D B Smith
The Granary
Mill Lane
Acaster Malbis
York YO23 2UL

ISBN 0 9539344 0 3

Produced, printed and bound by York Publishing Services Ltd, 64 Hallfield Road, Layerthorpe, York YO31 7ZQ.

Contents

Preface

This book has been written as part of the Acaster Malbis village celebrations commemorating the Millennium and is a history of the village to the year AD 2000.

It is the culmination of research by a group of local residents, the aim being to write a book that is both a worthwhile record and an informative and interesting read.

The group: Catrina Appleby, James Hall, Stan Shoobridge, David Smith, Geoffrey Smith and Carol Woollcombe.

Acknowledgements

We would like to thank all those who have helped in any way with the writing of this book. In particular we would like to thank the following people: Vivienne Baren, Mr & Mrs W Dale, Alan Jackson, Mr & Mrs D Proctor, Roger Raimes, Dorothy Reed, Mr & Mrs C A Robinson, Mrs E E Smith, Mrs G Tonkinson and Vernon Whistlecraft for the loan of objects and illustrations; Harold Smith for his piece on the Second World War; Lin Taylor for drawing the objects; and Geoff Appleby for his work on the Malbis and Fairfax documents.

We would like to thank Nigel and Charles Forbes Adam and the Escrick Park Estate for allowing us access to their family archives (Wenlock papers) held at the University of Hull Brynmor Jones Library and for permission to reproduce the 1763 map of the village.

We would also like to thank the staff of the Brynmor Jones Library for their help with the Wenlock papers; Mrs R Freedman and Mrs A Wheeler of York City Archives for transcribing the twelfth-century manuscript; Antonia Kershaw of English Heritage for her help with the aerial photographs; Dr Ailsa Mainman of York Archaeological Trust for identifying the Anglo-Saxon pot; J P G Taylor for information about Richard Thompson; Susie White of Liverpool University for her information about the clay pipes; Lynne Gray for the loan of her dissertation; Suffolk County Council Sites and Monuments Record for information on Eye, and John Oxley of York City Council for supplying us with maps.

Figures 6 and 10 are reproduced by kind permission of Mrs A Spokes Symmonds and A Crawshaw respectively.

We would like to thank Mr D Proctor for his generous donation towards the production costs of this book.

We are very grateful to Michelle Kendrick for her expert help in bringing this book to print.

Finally, we would like to thank the Acaster Malbis Millennium Committee for supporting the production of this book.

Illustrations

1

Introduction

Cruising south down the River Ouse from York on one of the many pleasure boats, the visitor sees the Archbishop's Palace at Bishopthorpe; beyond this to his right lies farmland, to his left Naburn Marina, with the prominent spire of Naburn church visible in the distance. Shortly after, the village of Naburn comes into view, and on the right bank, the Ship Inn at Acaster Malbis, just above Naburn Lock. For most people this is journey's end, but although many people know the name of Acaster Malbis, few can tell you anything about the village. It is however a village with a long and fascinating history.

Figure 1 Aerial view of Acaster Malbis, July 1999.

The parish of Acaster Malbis (SE 590 455) lies on the west bank of the River Ouse, some four miles south-west of York. A rural parish, covering *c* 1800 acres (750 hectares), its economy has long been based on farming and, to a lesser extent, fishing. Today that income is supplemented by the so-called leisure industry, primarily in the form of caravan sites, although even these can claim a longer history than most.

The land is generally flat, rising slightly from the river, and virtually the whole parish lies below the 10m contour. The eastern half of the parish lies on alluvium, what is locally referred to as 'light land', being a light, sandy soil over heavy clay.

Not surprisingly for such a low-lying parish, drainage is an important issue: every field is drained and much of the parish boundary is marked by drainage ditches of various sizes. To the west

1

lies the Foss, a canalised stream which runs south as far as Woolas Hall, near Appleton Roebuck where it joins the Fleet, another canalised stream which flows ultimately into the River Wharfe. To the east lies the River Ouse. Names such as 'Thomas Dyke' (on South Ings), first recorded in the thirteenth century, reflect the importance of dykes in the landscape.

The rather straggling village lies on the eastern edge of the parish, close to the Ouse. Today what might be called the 'main street' is Mill Lane, but in the eighteenth century the properties clustered around Moor End and along the river bank. The church of the Holy Trinity lies isolated to the north of the main village, on slightly higher ground above the river, opposite Naburn. Since it is thought that it originally served the three villages of Acaster Malbis, Bishopthorpe and Naburn, this may account for both its dedication and location. Over 400 acres (c 166ha) of Naburn land lay within the jurisdiction of Acaster Malbis parish until the late nineteenth century, parishioners crossing by ferry to attend services.

Much of the land within the parish is arable, but Church Ings and South Ings are permanent pasture. These areas of meadow land, which are subject to periodic flooding, were excluded from the enclosure process in the eighteenth century and continue to be held in multiple ownership.

Today the only significant area of woodland is Stub Wood, towards the southern end of the parish. The name Stub derives from 'stubb', meaning tree-stump and is first recorded in the thirteenth century. That the wood is of considerable antiquity is attested by the abundance of bluebells and wood anenomes.

One of the most unusual features of Acaster Malbis is that until the twentieth century almost the entire parish had passed through the hands of only three families since shortly after Domesday, which may account for the survival of certain customs in the village. The Malbis family acquired the estate by marriage in the twelfth century and late in the fourteenth century it passed to the Fairfaxes. In 1755 Viscount Fairfax sold it to Lady Sarah Dawes, the widow of Beilby Thompson of Escrick, the Thompson family holding it until 1898, when they were forced to sell during the agricultural depression. The estate then passed into multiple ownership, for perhaps the first time in its history.

Today the village consists of several small farms, five caravan parks, and housing, principally along Mill Lane and at Lakeside. Much of the housing development has occurred within the last twenty years, bringing many newcomers into the village. The presence of a pub, a church and a village hall, important features in any rural setting, help to ensure the survival of a village community.

2
The Camp by the River

Very little is known of the prehistory of Acaster Malbis, but a few flints show prehistoric man at least passed through the area as early as the Mesolithic age more than six thousand years ago, although he probably did not stay. During the Neolithic period (*c* 4000–2000 BC) two individuals had cause to regret their visit to Acaster: they lost their stone axes, valuable pieces of equipment. Other finds have included these thumb-nail scrapers, also Neolithic in date. The land at that time was probably heavily wooded and unattractive for farming.

It seems the Romans may have appreciated the strategic importance of the site, on a major bend in the river, as they sailed up the Ouse in the late first century AD. The name Acaster probably comes from the Old English word for a river, 'ea' (A), combined with 'ceaster', a fortification. Local tradition has long held that there was a Roman fort here, 'the fort on the river' referred to in the name, placing it in the Ship Inn area, close to the site of the original ferry, but no convincing evidence has ever been presented for it. It now seems more likely that the fort, if it existed, was located further south, just to the west of South Ings, an argument supported by a small scatter of Roman finds from this area. In the 1920s three Roman coins were discovered at the brickyard, a little further west. What was thought to be Roman masonry was discovered in a service trench near the Methodist chapel in 1965, but it was not recorded. The first centuries AD certainly saw settlement across the river in Naburn parish; here, recent excavations have revealed a number of Romano-British farmsteads dating from the first to the third century AD. The river was no doubt very busy during the Roman period, with ships bringing goods to supply the soldiers and civilians of the rapidly expanding town of Eboracum.

Settlement may well have continued in the post-Roman or Anglo-Saxon period since a near-complete wheel-thrown pot found in the brick pond in 1927 has recently been identified as being probably of

Figure 2 Mesolithic flint blades and Neolithic thumb-nail scrapers.

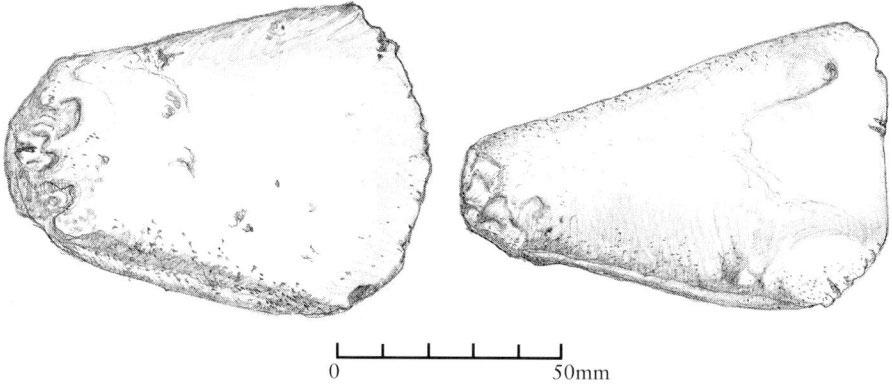

Figure 3 Neolithic stone axes.

Anglo-Saxon date. Viking spindle whorls, for spinning wool, have also been recovered from fields at the southern end of the village.

There is no written record of Acaster until the Domesday Book of 1086, but by this time there was clearly a proper village, as the entry records:

> In Acaster [Malbis] Alsige (had) 4 carucates of land taxable. Land for 2 ploughs.
> Now Robert has there 2 ploughs, and 3 villagers
> Value before 1066, 20s; now 15s.

Acaster survived the infamous 'Harrying of the North' in 1069–70, when much of northern England was laid waste by the Normans. This was almost certainly because the owner was either William Malet, King William's commander in the north, or his son Robert Malet (the Robert referred to in Domesday). Nearby Middlethorpe was not so lucky: it is described as 'Waste', with a value of only 3s (shillings); prior to the Conquest it too was valued at 20s.

Figure 4 Roman copper alloy coin of Augustus (27 BC – AD 14).

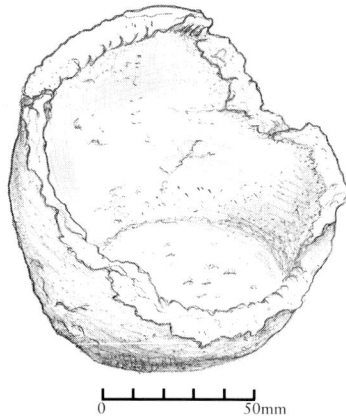

Figure 5 Wheel-thrown Anglo-Saxon pot, possibly a crucible.

The village almost certainly had a church by the late eleventh century since there are Norman capitals built into the east wall of the present church (which dates from the early fourteenth century) and an eleventh-century alabaster priest's tomb.

DOMESDAY

Following the Battle of Hastings in 1066 and the victory of William, Duke of Normandy (the Conqueror) over the Anglo-Saxon Harold Godwinson, the Norman system of land tenure based upon military service was introduced. The critical aim, from William's point of view, was to maintain his hold on his newly won lands, even though the Normans were in the minority. He did this by developing an effective and compact army which was supported by an assurance of loyalty made by his high-ranking feudal tenants. This was at the heart of the feudal system: land in return for service. On-going disputes about titles to land, especially with the bishoprics and abbeys, led, in 1086, to a huge sworn description, or inquest as it was called, being made into the wealth of the King's feudal tenants. This was intended by William to be not only a record of the holding of each of his tenants, but also a means of establishing the amount of income that he could extract by way of tax. Thus the Domesday Book was born.

Acaster Malbis, being in the north of England, was included in a sub-division of land known as a Wapentake; these had generally superceded the earlier administrative sub-division known as a Hundred. Domesday entries can be rather confusing; Acaster Malbis is listed under both Skyrack Wapentake, along with the nearby villages of (Middle) Thorpe and Acaster (Selby), but it is also recorded as being in Ainsty Wapentake. Fortunately both entries agree that Robert Malet held four carucates of land here.

A carucate of land was the amount of land which could be ploughed by a team of oxen in one year; this varied according to the type of land and its location but the average amount is thought to have been about 120 acres (50ha).

The annual income of William the Conqueror, exclusive of fines etc, has been computed at £400,000, an immense sum if the circumstances of the time are considered.

3
Three in One

Hidden amongst mature trees about a quarter of a mile from the main village lies the church of the Holy Trinity, on an island of higher ground above Church Ings. Its location and dedication have been the subject of much speculation over the years but the most likely explanation is that since the church probably served not only Acaster Malbis but also Naburn and Bishopthorpe originally, it was located on a convenient site for all parishioners. This might also account for the dedication. What is certain is that the villagers of Acaster have been worshipping on the same site for nearly nine hundred years.

We know for certain that there has been a church on this site since at least 1294, when Acaster Malbis is listed as paying Pope Nicholas' taxation. This first church may well have been built soon after the Conquest; the fact that there is no mention of a church in the Domesday Book entry doesn't mean there wasn't one: Domesday is notoriously unreliable on this.

Figure 6 Holy Trinity Church, 1966. (© Mr P S Spokes)

In the mid twelfth century both the village and the church passed into the hands of the family with whom it would forever be associated: the Malbis family (see Chapter 4).

In 1198, Richard de Malbysse founded the Premonstratensian abbey of Newbo, in Lincolnshire, endowing it with Acaster church and various other lands. This meant that the monks had the advowson, or 'gift of the living' (ie they could nominate the vicar who would then receive the salary for that parish). The monks were not always very strict, allowing the living to pass from father to son on payment of a fine. It should be remembered that this was the Catholic church, although at that time a two-tier clergy existed, drawing bishops from the monastic orders but allowing parish priests to marry and have children.

Surviving medieval documents tell us the names of several early vicars of Acaster Malbis: vicars are often listed as witnesses to legal documents because they were (usually) literate. The first recorded vicar is a John of Acaster, whose name appears in an early thirteenth-century document.

The fourteenth century is particularly well documented, thus we know that in 1335 the vicar was John de Sutton of the wealthy and important family Sutton of Holderness; his arms are in the east window of the church. In 1387 a land document refers to a Robert de Acastre, chaplain, and the witnesses include Dom Richard de Gram, vicar of Acaster. In 1388 Dom William Malbys is listed as chaplain while in 1389 John de Burton is described as clerk and vicar.

On 29 September 1507, Dom Symon Fereman specified that he was 'To be buried in the grave of the church of Holy Trinity'; he actually lived until 1519!

The monks at Newbo retained the living until the Dissolution of the Monasteries in 1538, when Acaster church passed to the Crown and then to the Fairfax family, who held the estate. In 1579 a Cuthbert Fairfax was granted the Rectory of Acaster for 21 years, but in 1590 a sequestration order was served against him and one Gabriel Squire on the grounds that there had been only one sermon that year. In 1597 however Squire was presented with the vicarage by the Queen!

By the mid eighteenth century Holy Trinity had been combined with St Andrew's, Bishopthorpe, a John Dealtary being granted the vicarage of Bishopthorpe and the perpetual curacy of Acaster Malbis until his death.

It seems that Acaster Malbis may well have been a centre for recusants, Catholics who refused to attend Church of England services. Recusancy was strong in Yorkshire in the late sixteenth and early seventeenth century and many notable Yorkshire families fought for the King in the Civil War. There are several references to members of the Fairfax family being non-communicants, people being encouraged to report on their neighbours. Thus the Visitation Book for York in 1594, compiled by Robert Scaife, notes that 'Mary Fairfax, wife of Cuthbert did not communicate at Easter', while that for 1596 notes that Peter Vavasour (then resident in the village) had his child baptised not in church but at home, 'by whom they know not'. The same Book also admonishes the church wardens, William Spinke and Richard Cawood, for having a broken alms chest.

It is thus not surprising to find that in 1619 Thomas Fairfax is fined 'for suffering the chancel to be ruinated in the roofe thereof and for not beautifying the said chancel within'. He was also accused of letting the church 'be in very great decay and like to fall down, and hurtfull to the people and like to bring the steeple downe'.

The fact that in 1764 the church was paying a 'poor boy' 2d for whipping out the dogs prior to Sunday service suggests the Fairfaxes had not maintained the building well during their tenure.

The Church

The present church building dates from the early fourteenth century, but there is evidence of an earlier Norman building. There must certainly have been a church of some kind in order that Pope Nicholas could tax it in 1294! This first church would have been small but it must have been built at least partially in stone since there are Norman capitals built into the east wall. There is also an early, possibly eleventh-century, priest's tomb, now located to the north of the altar. This tomb is of Derbyshire alabaster and may have been brought here by the monks of Newbo.

Built of Magnesian limestone in the early 1300s, the present church is said to have been designed by the monks at Newbo. It is meant to be cruciform in plan but something went slightly awry and the arms are of uneven lengths. One of the most unusual features is the central wooden bell tower (with two bells) and octagonal spire with wooden shingles. The church was heavily restored in 1886 by C Hodgson Fowler at a cost of over £1000. The present spire dates from this restoration, but the seventeenth-century report quoted above shows it had a 'steeple' then.

There were three altars, each with a piscina (stone basin), perhaps reflecting the symbolism of the Trinity, an unusual dedication 700 years ago. A document of 1471 records a chapel of St Mary within the church.

The church was heavily damaged during the Civil War when the Scots were quartered in the village, but some medieval stained glass survives, collected together at the bottom of the east window. The seven-light east window is attributed to Robert the Northumbrian, who was responsible for the great west window of York Minster in the fourteenth century.

To the south of the altar lies the remarkable tomb of Sir John de Malbysse (died 1316), with its life-size effigy of a knight with his legs crossed. This may have been erected first in the Norman church, before being moved to the new building. In the north transept lies a tombstone dated 1420, commemorating Nicholas Norfolk of Naburn and his wife Ellen Dawnay of Escrick.

Also medieval in date is the tub font, which rather strangely bears the mark of a padlock. This dates from the days of Sewell de Bovill, Archbishop of York in 1290; he ordered that all fonts should be kept locked as people were taking the water for 'unhallowed purposes'. Locking a font away from air, in the days when infants were baptised by total immersion, must have produced some unhallowed germs!

The ornate pulpit is seventeenth century in date and probably Flemish. In the same century Lord Fairfax financed the large Royal Arms, erected in honour of Charles II in 1683 after the failure of the Puritan-led Rye House Plot. It bears the unusual inscription 'Fear God, Honour the King', a reminder of the church's secular role. Originally sited in the vestry, the Arms were restored in memory of the postmistress Marian Shoobridge and are now located above the south-west door. In the north transept can be found the painted plaque of *c* 1764 recording the benefactions of John Knowles in 1603 (see p 22).

Until the mid nineteenth century, when a new church was built at Naburn, Acaster church served a large part of what is now Naburn parish. Parishioners would cross the river on the ferry to attend services, coffins being brought the same way, to be buried in the south side of the churchyard in an area allocated for Naburn residents. In the fifteenth century application had to be made to consecrate additional land in the churchyard.

Figure 7 Holy Trinity Spire. (© Lin Taylor)

The Vicarage

On 15 January 1348 the Archbishop of York ordained that the church at Acaster Malbis was to be provided with a perpetual vicar, one of the Canons of Newbo filling the post. This new post was almost certainly linked to the building of the new church and it is reasonable to suppose that the vicar was provided with a vicarage. There is no evidence to suggest that this was not the same site as that used for the new vicarage in 1732. A Terrier (land document) of 1716 records that the vicarage of Acaster Malbis was endowed with a dwelling house and orchard adjoining on the west side, being about 50 yards in length and about 20 in breadth. This would fit well with the known site. The value annually was put at 10s and the salary was £12 annually, payable half yearly at Michaelmas (29 September) and Lady Day (25 March). Out of this £12 the vicar had to provide the bread and wine, vestments and other ornaments of the altar – 'and shall be at the charge of washing them'.

The fees at that time were:

Marriage	2/6
Christening	Nil
Churching	8d
Burial with coffin	1/2
Burial without coffin	7d

Figure 8 Ann Darling and Emily Wentworth (nee Darling) outside the Old Vicarage, c 1875. At this time the building was the village shop, having for a while been the Fisherman's Arms.

The dwelling house mentioned in 1716 was probably of timber, since in 1732 a new vicarage was built from scratch at the sole expense of the then incumbent J Addison. The cost of £35 4s 8d amounted to three years full income of the Benefice of Living of the parish. The brick-built property, which originally had a thatched roof, included a garth to the rear, and the plot still survives today. A stone plaque near the door bears the inscription:

I.A.

1732

Æ 65

SIC VOS

NON VOBIS

These lines are taken from a longer quotation by Virgil and a precise translation is not really possible. The intended meaning however is 'We do things not entirely for ourselves', clearly a reference to his generosity in building the property.

The field adjacent to the vicarage was known by the name of Tyn Garth, which may derive from the word 'tithe' or tenth part. It is said that the foundation or base of the tithe barn was located in the garth *c* 1900.

By 1743 the house was let for 40s per annum (quite where the vicar was residing we do not know) and in 1786 the garth was let to farmland for £1 17s 0d. By 1818 the house had fallen into disrepair and was classed as 'unfit for residence', although it was later to enjoy a new life as a pub (!) and then the village shop (see Chapter 8).

The church also owned 34 acres (14ha) on the former Elvington Common, purchased for £200 from Queen Anne's Bounty, to augment the Living. This was not a good investment however on account of the 'extreme barrenness of the soil', and was later supplemented by more profitable land at Melbourne in the parish of Thornton which brought in £8 per annum. The parish was clearly a poor one since various grants were made during the eighteenth and nineteenth century to further augment the living, including £300 from Frances Lawley, MP, the Patron.

4

Of Malet, Malbis and Fairfax

A ttempting to unravel the history of the Malet, Malbis and Fairfax families in the eleventh to fourteenth centuries has been the most difficult part of this book. The Malet and Malbis families were Norman French in origin, arriving with William the Conqueror in 1066, although the latter do not appear in the village that takes their name until the mid twelfth century. Records for this period are sketchy but there is enough to tell us that the Malbis family were of some importance in the York area and they made some interesting marriages. Since all the principal characters seem to have been called either Richard or William, with the odd John thrown in for added interest, it gets very confusing at times! (The name Malbis appears in numerous variations, from Malebisse to Malbysse to Malbys.)

The problems get worse in the mid fourteenth century when the de Malbis family become entangled with the Fairfaxes, that most complicated of Yorkshire families. The Fairfax genealogy is notoriously difficult and the most widely accepted is still that produced by Joseph Foster in the late nineteenth century.

What the present research has shown is that the traditional story of Richard de Malbis' marriage to Maud of Acaster in 1198 is incorrect – if only it was that simple!

What follows is the story as far as we have been able to ascertain it in the time available, but many questions remain unanswered.

The name Malebisse (or a variant) first appears in the time of William I, when one Hugh de Malebisse held lands in York. By 1086 Acaster was held by Robert Malet, son of William Malet who was the tenant-in-chief following the Conquest. William, at one time the King's commander in the north, was the custodian of York castle.

The Malets held land not only in Yorkshire but also had large holdings around Eye in Suffolk; in 1210 Richard Malbysse is recorded as holding one knight's fee in the Honour of Eye. That fee consisted of lands at Acaster and Newbo in Lincolnshire, of which more later. This and other evidence suggests that there may have been a connection by marriage between the Malet and Malebisse families.

In 1106 Robert Malet was killed at the Battle of Tinchenbrai, fighting for Robert, Duke of Normandy and as a result his heirs were dispossessed by Henry I. Sometime in the early twelfth century the Malbis family acquired parts of Robert Malet's land, the first recorded holder being William Malebisse who died in 1176. William's father was Hugh Malebisse, the steward of Roger de Mowbray, one of the most important landlords in Yorkshire. William married into another important family – the Percys. He married Emma de Percy, an illegitimate daughter of William Percy, but she was clearly an accepted member of the family, as she brought a dowry which included lands in Acaster. We know this from a twelfth-century document recently discovered in York City Archives (M61):

> Know ye as well present as future that I William Malebisse have given and granted to Robert Neve for the service that he did to me and for homage, two bovates of land in Acaster that William, son of Pagan held to him and his heirs, to hold of me and my heirs in hereditary fee, namely in wood, plain, meadow, field and pasture with all its appurtenances rendering annually one pound of pepper at Christmas. This also I have done by grant and gift of Lady Emma my spouse of whose dower that land is and by grant of Richard Malebisse my eldest son and heir, the above-named pound of pepper he will give to me for all service that to the above-named land belongs free and quit from all services due to me and my heirs. These being witnesses Robert Malebisse, Hugo Malebisse, Osbert Malebisse, Jeffrey Barr, Nigel de Flabourch, Robert son of Jeffrey Malebisse, William Malebisse, Hugo Malebisse, Alexander Barre, Robert de Auvers, Robert le Mansel and many others.

The original twelfth-century document is remarkably well preserved, the Latin being clear and (fairly) easy to read. The rent of a pound of pepper was not uncommon – a similar document refers to a pound of cumin – spices being extremely valuable. It is from payments such as this that we get the term 'peppercorn rent'. The witnesses to the document read like a roll-call of the Malebisse family. Unfortunately the document is not dated, but it must be before 1176 as we know that is when William Malebisse died.

Emma de Percy had a legitimate half-sister called Maud. She married the third Earl of Warwick before 1175, becoming the Countess of Warwick. Her husband died childless in 1184 and she agreed to pay the huge sum of 700 marks (£233 6s 8d) in order to recover her dowry and to be free to marry whom she wished. (Her heirs were still repaying the debt ten years after her death.) One possibility, although we have no proof, is that she married a Malebisse and she is the 'Lady Maud Malebys' referred to in an early thirteenth-century document. This Lady Maud also had land in Acaster in her dowry.

Alternatively, there may genuinely have been a Maud, daughter of Robert de Acaster, who married a Malebisse, as the original story goes ...

There certainly was an Acaster family at this time and they by no means died out after the Malebisse family took control, their name appearing frequently in documents throughout the thirteenth and fourteenth century. In 1252 Robert, son of John de Acaster is listed as holding lands at Thorp [Middlethorpe], while a John de Acastre witnesses several documents in the 1370s. He must have died soon after however since in 1380, one 'Isolda' is described as 'wife of the late John de Acastre'. In June 1387 a document refers to Robert de Acastre, chaplain, and Richard Malbys, lord of Acaster.

To return to William Malebisse – he and Emma had five sons, the eldest of whom, Richard, was a major figure in Yorkshire in the late twelfth and early thirteenth century. Of Hugh, Roger and Geoffrey (Jeffrey) we know virtually nothing, but William jnr probably held lands in Cleveland and was Lord of the Manor at Ayton, where he built a chapel in 1215. William Malebisse died in 1176, probably on Crusade, at which point Richard succeeded to his lands.

Richard is one of the most colourful (and notorious) members of the Malebisse family and we know quite a lot about him. Firstly, he too married a lady whose dowry included land in Acaster, a lady called Elena. This brings to three the number of Malebisse marriages which brought them land in Acaster, suggesting love was probably not the principal motive driving the Malebisse men!

In the 1180s Richard was Lord Chief Forester of Galtres, Derwent and Wernerdale, and had extensive estates in Yorkshire, although he seems to have been in financial difficulties as early as 1182. Soon after the accession of Richard I in 1189 he was appointed the Chief Justice of Assize, but the title was short-lived, since in 1190 he was one of the principal figures in the notorious Jewish Massacre in York. For this he gained the nickname 'Mala Bestia' and was fined £40. After the Massacre Richard became involved in a conspiracy with Richard I's brother, John (later King), for which he was excommunicated in 1191 and fined 300 marks three years later. In 1194 Richard and his co-conspirators (among them William Percy jnr) were allowed to take up their lands again under licence, pending the King's return. With John's accession in 1199, Richard took full control of his lands again but only after paying another fine, this time of £100, two morris-hawks, two leashes of harriers and four palfreys (a type of horse).

Not surprisingly, Richard's plans to fortify his house at Wheldrake in 1200 were not well received and they were never implemented. He presumably maintained a residence at Acaster as well.

Richard and Elena had three children, John, Richard and Emma. We know John married a lady called Matilda and they had a son, William. In the mid 1300s this William married another Matilda, probably a member of the Neville family, another important northern family.

By 1198 Richard de Malebisse had large possessions, including Acaster, and in that year he founded the Premonstratensian monastery of Newbo, in Lincolnshire, granting it, amongst other lands, the church at Acaster. These grants were confirmed by Richard's son, John, in 1213, following the death of his father in 1210.

The site of the abbey of the Blessed Virgin Mary at Newbo lies between Barrowby and Sedgebrook in north Lincolnshire. The monastery was small, with never more than thirteen canons, and in 1401 it was almost depopulated by the results of 'pestilence and poverty'. It survived, but was never wealthy; in 1534, two years before it was dissolved, the annual revenue was £71 8s 11d, including the rectory of Acaster Malbis. The abbey was dissolved in 1536, when it had an abbot, six canons and a novice. A few earthworks are all that remain today.

The Malebisse family continue to crop up regularly in the thirteenth century, usually making grants of land to various priories. In the early 1300s another Richard appears, paying 10s 8d as aid to Edward I in 1303 and listed as a *miles* [soldier] of Edward II in 1310. In 1314 John, Lord Malebisse, perhaps Richard's brother, is *vice comes Ebor*, the High Sheriff of York. This is the Sir John de Malebisse whose effigy lies in Acaster Malbis church, who died in 1316.

Sir John Malebisse was succeeded by his son William, who was a knight by 1336. In 1341 William was in financial difficulty and was forced to 'mortgage' his Acaster lands, although only for the duration of his life; his eldest son, also William, retained his inheritance. The terms of the deal were that Sir William would receive 40 marks immediately, with a further 100 marks to come. His son William was married to a lady called Isabel and at that time they were living in Filey. Sir William had two more sons, Thomas and John, and probably a daughter, Margaret.

Sometime *c* 1340 Margaret Malebisse, the grand-daughter of Lord John, married Thomas Fairfax. She did not take with her the Acaster lands, although from that time on the Fairfaxes began to quarter their arms with those of the Malebisses, as can be seen in the Great Hall at Gilling Castle.

The precise legal grounds for the transfer of the Acaster lands to the Fairfaxes remains unclear. It is usually suggested that they acquired it by marriage, but the evidence seems to suggest otherwise. Records of Malebisse/Fairfax marriages in the fourteenth century are very confusing; the Malebisse females are scattered at random amongst the various Fairfaxes, over several generations. The two families undoubtedly did inter-marry but the inheritance of the manor of Acaster Malbis is much more complex than a simple marriage!

Sir William snr died probably in the late 1340s and was succeeded by Margaret's brother, Sir William jnr, who had two sons, Thomas and Walter. Thomas, the elder, was a soldier who died sometime between 1362 and 1365, predeceasing his father. He left a daughter, Elizabeth, who married Adam de Beckwith. Walter, the younger son, had gone on pilgrimage to the Holy Land, mortgaging his lands at Scalton to William Fairfax and making Richard Fairfax, William's son, his heir if he did not return.

When Sir William Malebisse died in 1365 it was assumed that Walter had died in the Holy Land, and there followed a most unholy scramble for his lands, two of the principal claimants being a Sir William de Seint Quintyn and his wife Dame Elizabeth, presumably Walter's niece who had remarried. Walter had not died however and returned to claim his lawful inheritance. A law suit was brought against Sir William and Dame Elizabeth, who are described as being in possession of the manor of Acaster Malbis by 'right heritage' of Elizabeth. The outcome of the suit is not known but in 1368 Sir William de sancto Quentin grants the entire manor to William Fairfax.

The Fairfaxes then conduct a very confusing series of legal moves, the motive for which remains obscure. William Fairfax transfers the manor of Acaster to his brother John, Rector of Gilling. John then grants the manor to Richard, William's son, in return for him rendering military service and adopting the Malbis name. On the death of Rector John, the inheritance passes to his elder nephew Thomas (d 1394) and then to Richard Fairfax, Thomas' son.

When Richard 'Malbis' (Fairfax) dies on 1 November 1401, Richard Fairfax descends upon Acaster and seizes the manor, evicting Richard Malbis' widow Isabella and son William (who was then aged nine and thus unable to render military service). Isabella remarries to Nicholas Saxton and in 1402 initiates a series of lawsuits to try and re-establish her son's claim. The legal wranglings continued, at great expense, until 1407 but in the end she lost the case.

In 1414 William Malbis came of age and was therefore able to inherit the tenancy! William was married at the tender age of nine to Sybil Neville, and after his early death in 1426, she began a further series of lawsuits against Richard Fairfax. Once again Richard Fairfax won and from then on the inheritance of the Acaster lands seems not to have been in dispute.

The manor of Acaster Malbis continued to be held directly from the King as part of the Honour of Eye, in return for military service, into the sixteenth century, being recorded in the will of Thomas Fairfax, knight, who died on 31 March 1505, when it was worth £45.

It seems that its status as part of the Honour of Eye conferred certain privileges, not least the exemption of its tenants from paying tolls etc 'in all cities ... in England'. In 1452 Henry Gascoigne is called upon to provide evidence as to why his tenants in Naburn are not paying their tolls. Gascoigne argues that the land, which he rents from William Fairfax for 4s a year, is part of the manor of Acaster Malbis, which is part of the Eye fee (a parcel of land) known as the 'Malbyssh fee'.

5

Between Lidgate and Gevemersc

By the fourteenth century Acaster Malbis was a proper village, a total of 44 people paying the Poll Tax of 1379 (see Appendix 1). It had a church, a manor house and a main street ranged along the river bank, very much as is shown on the map of 1763 (see Fig 11 on p 28). It is thus disappointing to find that there are no remains of the medieval village surviving today other than the church, although large quantities of medieval pottery have been recovered from the fields at the south end of the parish.

Immediately to the south in the parish of Acaster Selby lies the site of St Andrew's College. This, a secular college, was founded in 1470 by Robert Stillington, a native of Acaster Selby who was then Bishop of Bath and Wells. The College had a provost and three priests acting as schoolmasters. The College was dissolved *c* 1548, although a William Gegoltson remained as master and curate to the residents of Acaster Selby. Edward VI then endowed a grammar school at Giggleswick, which still exists today, with the possessions of the College. Today there are the remains of the moat surrounding an island *c* 60m across, as well as the footings of the main College buildings to the south.

Two other moated sites are known in the area: Woolas Hall, which was probably a grange of St Mary's Abbey in York, lies to the west of the airfield and is now largely filled in; while Brocket Hall, to the east of Appleton Roebuck village, is a well-preserved double moat.

No trace now survives of the former preceptory of the Knights Templar in Copmanthorpe parish. The house, which was founded in 1258, lay to the north of Temple Lane and a preceptor is recorded in 1292 but not in 1308, suggesting the site was short-lived, although the memory lives on in several place-names.

By this time the Malbis family was well established in the village, to the extent that the village now bore their name. They would have had a manor house here, probably facing south on to Hauling (Hall) Lane, with stables and other ancillary buildings approximately where the Ship Inn now stands. There is a long-standing story of a moated manor house at Acaster but it now seems likely that the so-called moat was almost certainly some of the numerous drainage dykes which formerly existed in the Moor End area, particularly down towards the river, these dykes being commonly referred to as moats in the nineteenth century. The area between the Ship Inn and what is now Garth Farm has been so heavily remodelled in the last two hundred years as to remove any archaeological evidence that may once have existed.

Nineteenth-century antiquarians described a motte and bailey castle at Acaster, in the area of Garth Farm; indeed in the 1920s there were bus trips from York to view the 'ruins', but again there is no evidence on the ground to support this idea.

The villagers would have looked out onto a river teeming with traffic: in the days before proper roads, rivers were the quickest and most efficient means of transport for goods of all types. Boats and barges would have brought their cargoes, both foreign and local, up to York, then probably the most important town in northern England, while fishermen hauled salmon from the water. Until the construction of the weir in 1757 the Ouse was tidal as far as Boroughbridge, and boats would have to wait for the tide to bring them up the river.

In 1265 William Malebysse granted four acres of meadow (pasture) 'which abut the Linlands' to the monks at Rievaulx, specifying that the monks had free ingress and egress for carrying away the hay and 'for loading and unloading their ships ... between Lidgate and Gevemersc'. We cannot locate these lands precisely but the name Linlands probably refers to land where flax was grown and a site on either Church or South Ings seems likely.

To the west of the main street would have lain the village's open fields, although this is perhaps a confusing image as the parish was still heavily wooded at that time. The open-field system existed over much of England: the land was divided into a number of large fields, each of which was subdivided into furlongs and then strips, which were separated by a double furrow. The villagers each held a number of strips, spread amongst the fields to ensure not only that they each had their fair share of good and poor land but also that they had enough land from which to feed themselves, since one field would be left fallow each year to regain its fertility and to provide pasture for the animals.

When land changed hands, the land was described in terms of who held the adjoining strips: in 1358 William Malbys and his son Walter granted to William del Hall of Acastre '2 acres and half a rood of meadow in the south meadows of Acastre, lying next to the meadow of the abbot and convent of Rievall' on the south.

Farming was done communally – all the strips in one furlong would be planted with the same crop and sowing or harvesting would be done on agreed dates. Today medieval ridge and furrow underlies much of the permanent grassland around the village.

In most areas all remnants of the open-field system were swept away at enclosure, principally in the eighteenth century, but in Acaster Malbis there is a rare survival on the South Ings.

Acaster Ings

In the north of England Ings is a common name for a meadow or field, especially one by the side of a river. The term probably originated from the Old Norse word 'eng'. There are two main areas of Ings land in Acaster, South Ings and Church Ings, both of which are used for the production of hay and for the grazing of stock.

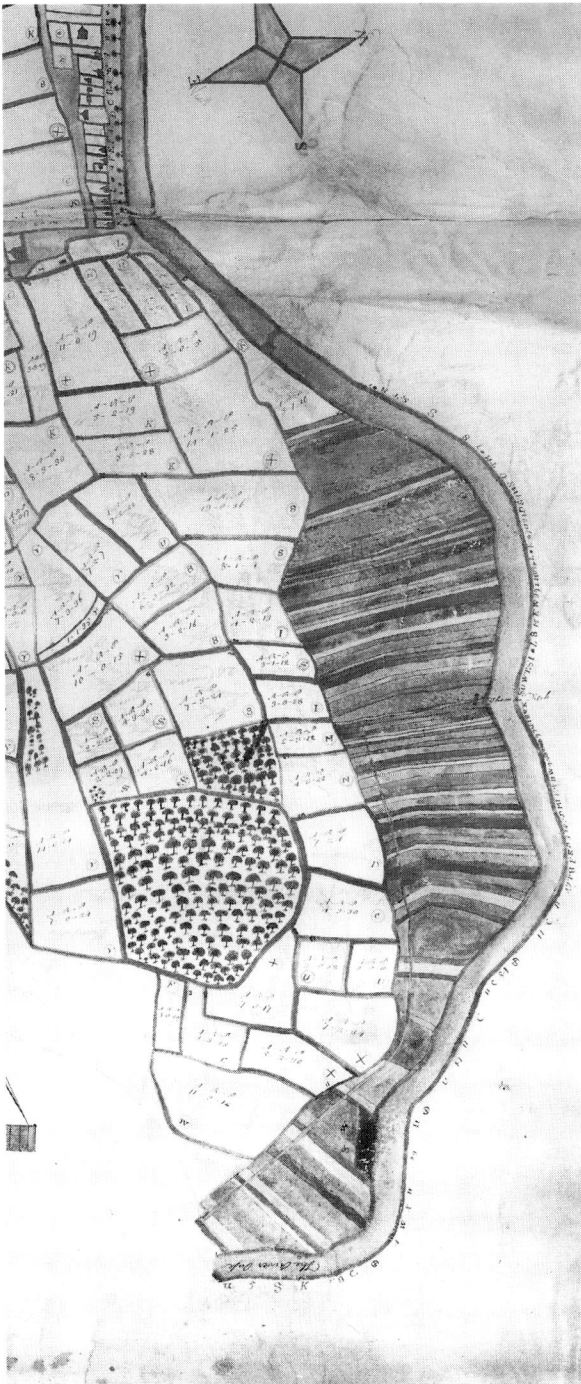

Figure 9 South Ings as shown on 1763 estate map. Each strip is identified, together with the tenant.

South Ings commences just below the weir at Naburn Lock and follows the river almost to Acaster Selby, covering *c* 110 acres (*c* 46ha). Although it is one large field separated only by Thomas Dyke, it is still in divided ownership amongst many of Acaster's farmers. The Ings were not enclosed when the rest of the parish was in the later eighteenth century and each strip is recorded on the 1763 estate map, together with its tenant. Historically, the farmers who hold land on the Ings are called the 'Ings Masters', and the boundaries for their sections of land are indicated by marker posts or 'mere stones'. The Ings Masters have always maintained a record book listing their rules, regulations and minutes of meetings. The current one dates from 1899, the year after Lord Wenlock sold the Acaster Estate. Prior to this date the Ings administration and accounts were recorded in the Court Leet manorial records (see below).

Flooding is a common occurrence on the Ings during the winter months and attempts have been made in the past to try and prevent this happening. The raising of the banks and the construction of a flood barrier or 'clough', which traverses the field

Figure 10 Church Ings in flood, January 1986. (© A Crawshaw)

close to the entrance, have helped, but alas these have not always been enough. The Court Leet records indicate that on 14 July 1826 £1 of their expenses was used to provide ale to refresh the men who were examining and raising the river banks to help prevent flooding. Their efforts proved to be futile however as 'the Ings were lost' (ie flooded) later the same day, an unusual time of the year for this to happen. The loss of the Ings would have been a serious catastrophe for the village, since the hay crop would have been ready for cutting. No hay crop meant no winter fodder for the animals.

As the South Ings has always been farmed in a non-intensive manner there fortunately remains an interesting range of flora; this was considered important enough to try and preserve and it was granted the status of Site of Special Scientific Interest (SSSI) in April 1988. Restrictions imparted by this agreement cover such matters as the time of year when the hay can be harvested, the use of chemical sprays and fertilisers and the times of the year when stock are allowed to graze.

Church Ings, as the name suggests, lies to the rear of Holy Trinity and is approximately 50 acres (c 20ha) in size, of which about sixteen acres is covered by an SSSI agreement. These Ings are still sometimes referred to as the Ferry Fields as it was from down here that the cross-river ferry from Naburn at one time operated.

In the nineteenth century a wind pump was installed by Lord Wenlock in an attempt to help purge the Ings of its flood water. The Acaster Internal Drainage Board has since replaced the wind pump with an electric one, but the building remains fairly intact, with some of the original mechanism inside. The sails unfortunately have long disappeared (see Fig 14 on p 34).

The Court Leet

The Court Leet was the medieval manorial court, presided over by the Lord of the Manor. This court usually met twice a year and was a form of local government. Failure to turn up for jury service at the court could result in a fine of up to 10s in the mid nineteenth century, while using abusive language to a fellow juryman resulted in a fine of 10/6d. In Acaster the Court Leet survived until the Great Sale of 1898 (see p 56), probably because the estate had remained intact. It dealt with minor crimes, controlled the sale and inheritance of land and defined the agricultural practices of the village. These included crops to be grown, harvesting days and the number of days to be worked by each tenant.

The court held an annual dinner, given by the Lord of the Manor; at one time this was held in the upstairs room at the Fisherman's Arms (see below). The last dinner was held at the Ship Inn in 1913.

6
Of Charity and War

The Knowles Education Foundation

At the beginning of the seventeenth century the parish of Acaster Malbis was fortunate to be bequeathed a sum of money to assist in the education of the parishioners' children. In a will dated 18 August 1603, John Knowles of York, a yeoman formerly of Acaster Malbis, left the sum of £100 to be administered by four trustees who were instructed to find a suitable schoolmaster, 'a sufficient single man' to teach the children at a salary of £9 per annum, payable at May Day and Martinmas. The schoolmaster was not to undertake any other employment and the parishioners were not to contribute to his salary in any way.

Knowles also bequeathed £30 to the four trustees to provide for continual loans to be made at the beginning of each year to fifteen of the poorest of the Lord's tenants; it was intended that the £30 would generate an income of 36 shillings. The 36 shillings was to be loaned equally between the tenants and was to be repaid at the end of the same year. Surprisingly, none of the tenants were ever in such indigent circumstances as to require or accept the benefit of the trust.

In 1658 the trustees decided to purchase two small paddocks in Bootham, adjoining the city of York, commonly known as Bootham Garths or Coaters Closes and the rent received from this land was then used to pay the schoolmaster's salary.

This arrangement continued successfully for the next 167 years until 1825, when the trustees let the land on a 99-year building lease. It was leased to Thomas Bell, a builder, and William Bellerby, a joiner. The conditions of the lease were that they would build two good houses worth £2000 and that they should pay the Trust £36 annually. The houses were built and were situated on what is today Bootham Crescent. As the 99-year lease came to an end it fortunately coincided with a road-widening scheme by York City Council and the trustees were advised to sell. The money raised from this sale was subsequently invested in bonds and shares, as it still is today, and the income generated from these investments is used for the awarding of grants.

Church records reveal an unfortunate event in 1735: all four trustees died without appointing any successors, so the village appealed to the Recorder of York as to who should be the next four trustees. It was his opinion that the power to nominate four new trustees was vested in the heir of the last surviving trustee but he himself could not become one. This responsibility lay with a gentleman called John Doughty, whose name appears frequently in eighteenth-century records of the village.

The Knowles trustees were entrusted with a further bequest following the death of John Kettlewell on 14 March 1839. Kettlewell left £100 to be invested with the purpose of increasing the allowances of the aged poor of the parish but on no account was any money to be directed towards the employment of the schoolmaster.

The present-day Knowles Foundation has changed slightly and is now governed by a scheme made in 1930 by the Board of Education under the Charitable Trusts Act. There are now eight trustees to administer the grants and these are awarded only to 'young persons residing in the ancient parish of Acaster Malbis', which includes part of the village of Naburn as it was once part of the original ecclesiastical parish. The trustees hold meetings three times a year to discuss grants which are awarded to fund a variety of aspects of a young person's educational development, including activities such as music, sports, apprenticeships and field trips.

To think that the Foundation was established before the Gunpowder Plot and is still going strong today is a reflection of the careful control and prudent investments exercised by the previous trustees. John Knowles probably never imagined that his act of charity would still be of benefit to the children of Acaster Malbis nearly four centuries later.

The Civil War

Acaster Malbis played its own small but not insignificant part in that great upheaval which dominated British history in the seventeenth century – the English Civil War – which pitched Parliament against the Crown, in the form of King Charles I, for the government of the country. This rebellion reached a peak in 1642–6 and culminated in the execution of the King in 1649. The monarchy was not restored until 1660. The Siege of York was an important milestone in this struggle because possession of the city was of prime importance to both sides.

The summer of 1644 saw York besieged by three Parliamentarian armies. The East Midlands troops commanded by the Earl of Manchester held the line from Clifton, upstream of York, eastwards to the Foss at Layerthorpe; Oliver Cromwell was his second in command. The local Yorkshire Roundheads commanded by Lord Fairfax held the line from Layerthorpe to Fulford, downstream of York. Scottish troops commanded by the Earl of Leven held the half circle from Poppleton on the west bank of the Ouse upstream of York to Acaster Malbis. The city was held for the King by the Marquis of Newcastle.

It is reported that the Scottish troops, under the veteran Earl of Leven, were remarkably well officered as nearly every Colonel had served in the Continental Wars. A bridge of boats was constructed across the river at Acaster Malbis, linking Fairfax's headquarters with those of the Earl of Leven at Middlethorpe.

The Scots were very expensive people to keep since they were generally regarded with disdain by the English Parliamentary forces and were often allotted the least supplies, the worst quarters and received hardly any pay. Acaster Malbis was one of the villages in which they were quartered, and according to Fairfax correspondence 'they laid waste to all the corn and ate all the sheep, kine [cattle] and swine to the value of £2000'. The severity of the loss was such that Parliament introduced legislation whereby another Fairfax, the unfortunate landlord young Viscount Fairfax of Gilling, was obliged to forgive his Acaster tenants a whole year's rent.

No hard evidence of the Scottish troops' stay in the area remains although it is said that the old blacksmith's shop near the present Ship Inn was used as an armoury.

7

A New Owner

B y the early fifteenth century the estate was firmly in the hands of the Fairfaxes and there then followed a long period of stability. Documents suggest that at least part of the family were resident in the village, presumably in the manor house on Hauling Lane. Some were regular attenders at church, but the family seems to have had divided loyalties: some were clearly recusants (see p 7), but during the Civil War, Lord Fairfax commanded the Parliamentarian forces, while in 1683 the then Lord Fairfax financed the large Royal Coat of Arms in the church.

In 1755 all this was to change: for the first time in its history, the Acaster Malbis estate was formally sold. The vendor was one Charles, Viscount Fairfax and the purchaser was Dame Sarah Dawes, widow of Beilby Thompson of Escrick. The reason for the sale was simple: Fairfax wished to raise a substantial sum of money in order to build a large house in the centre of York, namely Fairfax House in Castlegate, one of the finest buildings of the period in the city.

The sale documents survive in the Wenlock archives at Hull University and reveal that Lady Sarah paid £26,000 for the estate, the sale being completed on 11 October 1755, with £10,000 paid immediately and the remaining £16,000 to be paid 25 March 1756, with interest. (For details of the Wenlock archives, see Appendix 2.)

The sale brought about two immediate changes in the village: firstly the manor house probably went out of use, Lady Sarah continuing to reside on the Escrick estate; and secondly, the parish's open fields were enclosed, resulting in a fine map by John Stodart in 1763 (see p 28).

In 1773 Lady Sarah died; in her will dated 29 October 1765 she granted to her 'Younger son Richard [the] principal sum of Two thousand pounds as his portion under and by virtue of his late father's marriage settlement', and in addition, in order to make 'more ample provision' for him, the Acaster Malbis Estate. Richard's elder brother Beilby Thompson obviously inherited the bulk of the Escrick estate, while his sister received a sum of £5700 invested in 'South Sea Annuities'. In retrospect Richard may well have got the best deal. The will states that Lady Sarah wished to avoid disputes between her two sons, suggesting their relationship may not always have been harmonious. There then followed a somewhat turbulent period in the history of the estate, although the villagers were probably not even aware of it.

Richard was something of a 'Black Sheep' in the Thompson family, like many younger sons at that time. He loved drinking and gambling and was a womaniser. He spent much of his time on the continent. When at home he loved to go hunting with his brother and George Palmes of Naburn in the woods on his Acaster estate. The men crossed the river on the Naburn ferry, paying the ferryman the sum of one shilling.

By 1778 Richard was in serious financial difficulty, borrowing £1000 from his brother, in addition to £1800 already borrowed in 1776. These are the sums we know of: the IOUs survive, but who knows how much more there was? Perhaps Beilby Thompson's patience ran out, for in March 1778 Richard passed the Acaster Estate to his brother and one James Hamlyn of Clovelly Court in Devon, through a process known as Lease and Release. This allowed the estate to be held 'In Trust', pending its sale, the proceeds of the sale to be used to discharge Richard's many debts. A buyer had not been found by 14 April 1778 however and Richard was desirous of raising a mortgage on it. Thompson and Hamlyn agreed, with a limit of £10,000, and on condition that they retained control of the money in order to discharge Richard's debts.

The property market was clearly not good at that time, since eleven years later the estate had neither been sold nor mortgaged. By then 'Richard Thompson having out of his own Monies paid and discharged the several debts and sums of money … due and owing from him', now wished to have his estate returned to him. Thus on 26 May 1789 he asked Thompson and Hamlyn to reconvey it to him for the sum of ten shillings. Quite how such a change in fortune came about remains a mystery.

In the late eighteenth century Richard was doing his bit for 'King and Country' during the Napoleonic War. Like many of the gentry, he raised a regiment of volunteers, which rejoiced in the name of the Ouse and Derwent Volunteer Infantry. 'Volunteers' were recruited from local villages and no doubt some men from Richard's Acaster estate joined up. The regiment survived until 1810, its end being marked by a grand dinner.

Richard was to hold the estate until his death, outliving his brother by more than twenty years. He never married but the final codicil to his will, dated 23 February 1820, only around six months before he died, granted an annuity of £1500 to a Marie Francoise Bidgrain 'of the same place [Grosvenor Square, London] and residing with the said Richard Thompson', which was to be paid out of the 'Manor or Lordship of Acaster Malbis'.

Probate was obtained on Richard's will on 15 September 1820. In it he made bequests to various people although the bulk of his estate passed to his nephew Paul Beilby Lawley. The will also made provision for laying out £22,000 in making a canal from Stillingfleet to Wheldrake (another part of the Escrick estate) to join the Rivers Derwent and Ouse, an ambitious project that was never completed.

1763 Estate Map

One of the most important recent discoveries has been a late eighteenth-century estate map held in the Wenlock archives. The map was drawn up by John Stodart in 1763 for Lady Sarah Dawes. It seems likely that the map was commissioned for the purpose of enclosure, although there is no proof. In most parishes the open fields were enclosed through an Act of Parliament, but in those parishes that were held entirely by one estate this was not necessary. The enclosure of a parish is of great significance because from that time the land ceased to be farmed communally and the former open fields were divided up, creating the field pattern we recognise today. The resulting individual fields were then divided between the various landowners or tenants.

The Acaster Malbis map has every field marked, with the tenant of each field identified through a key at the bottom, thus providing us with a list of tenants in 1763 (see Appendix 1). The identification of this as an enclosure map is supported by the fact that the Thompson family were busy enclosing their lands on the east bank of the Ouse in the 1750s.

The map is well drawn and appears fairly accurate, the only obvious error being that the compass sign is drawn back-to-front (a little worrying for a surveyor!). The map is extremely important, providing us with valuable information about two aspects of the village in the mid eighteenth century: the village layout and the land holdings on the Ings.

Each individual property in the village is identified on the map and reveals a layout rather different from today. At that time the properties clustered around Moor End and along the river bank, facing the footpath now known as Cobbler's Trod. The map reveals no fewer than eighteen properties along this path but the majority were abandoned sometime in the early 1800s, probably as a result of increased flooding after the construction of the weir in the 1750s. What is almost certainly the site of the original manor house is shown on the corner of Hauling Lane, behind the present Ship Inn. On the same plot, a notably large one, is a smaller building on the approximate site of the Inn. Local tradition records that this was the site of the stables for the manor, a suggestion well supported by the map.

The area of the village that appears to have undergone the most significant change is Moor End. The majority of the present properties are less than a hundred years old, notable exceptions being Dimple Cottage, Chestnut Farm and Portland Cottage. The map reveals a lane that is now almost completely gone, although its name survived until the early twentieth century. Ned Lane ran from Cowper Lane, to the north of what is now The Laurels, along the side of the Ciss Dyke, then east towards the river, through land that remained almost marshland until drained in recent times. Ned Lane joined the present Acaster Lane at what is termed 'Ciss Dike Brig'. The Moor End properties stood almost on an island, the majority it would appear facing onto Ned Lane, despite the dyke. The first half of the lane still survives, as an area of waste ground behind Lodge Farm, but the second half has been lost. For some reason the lane was the subject of controversy, since in a list of Pains (rules) for 1846, no.16 states that 'no person whatever make a Road

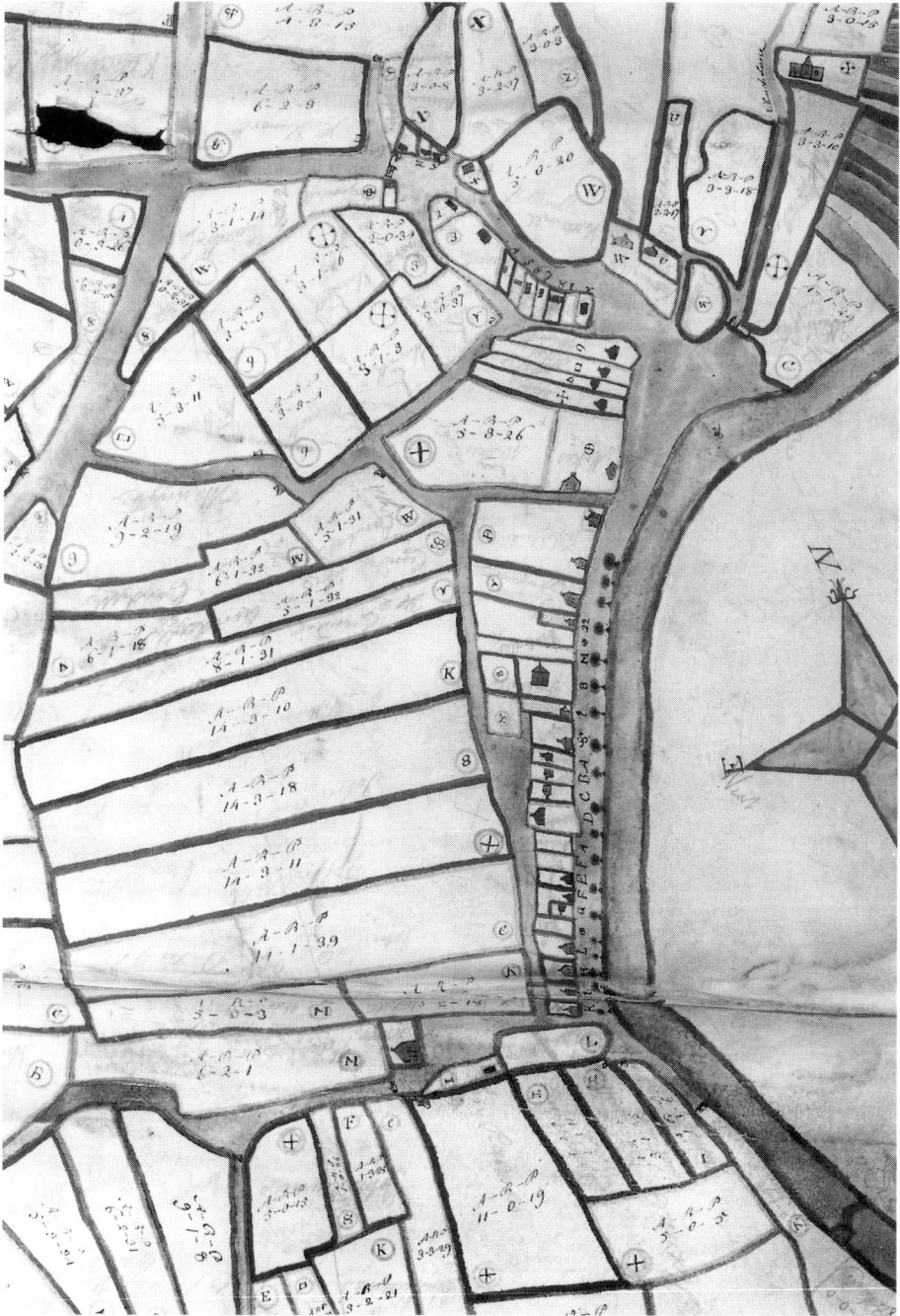

Figure 11 Extract from a Map of the Lordship of Acaster Malbys belonging to Lady Dawes, *J Stodart, 1763. (DDFA/45/4)*

from Siss Bridge up John Elsworth's fields to the Four Lane Ends. Any Trespasser detected to pay a fine of 5/-'.

The map includes a fine depiction of a large windmill situated in a field to the west of Acaster Lane, between the church and Bridge Farm. This was later dismantled and re-erected at the far end of Mill Lane, in what is now the Old Post Office caravan site, opposite Mill Cottage. Mill Lane at that time was purely a back lane, without any properties facing onto it. At the south end of the village, Manor Farm is shown as a building of some size, the building on the north side of the road being much larger than that which later became Southmoor House (now the Manor Guest House).

Figure 12 Post Mill near Bridge Farm shown on 1763 estate map.

Although the present road layout can be traced quite easily on the map, there are a number of areas where the roads appear to broaden out, eg at the old Green, at the area later known as Bakehouse Hill, and what is now the orchard to Manor Farm. These areas were known as 'Lord's Waste', having not been allocated during the enclosure process. Gates are shown at a number of points including: Acaster Lane, just beyond the church; adjacent to Manor Farm; Moor End; and at two points on the Appleton road. There are reports that Acaster Lane originally turned south-west, away from the river, opposite the church, running straight to Moor End, but there is no indication of this on the map. The map has what is probably the first depiction of the weir, which was constructed in 1757.

One of the most notable features is the depiction of the two Ings areas. Each of these is shown divided into numerous strips, each strip being separately coloured and the tenant identified. This shows quite clearly that the Ings were excluded from the enclosure process and continued to be held communally.

Prior to 1763, only a few small parcels of land seem to have been enclosed by the villagers, in contrast to the Thompsons' home village of Escrick. These 'closes' were generally created out of woodland or waste beyond the open fields and seem to have been held on a lease-hold type of arrangement, the land being bought and sold on the open market while the estate retained the freehold and ultimate control. Documents of the eighteenth and nineteenth century reveal these closes to have been on the outskirts of the parish, at Foss Closes, Nova Scotia and North Moor.

Woodland

The map of 1763 presents a slightly misleading picture of the village in the late eighteenth century. Perhaps because its primary purpose was to define field boundaries, it gives little indication as to the nature of the land. One might easily draw the conclusion that Acaster Malbis looked very much as it does today: a series of open fields, defined largely by hedges, with the only proper 'wood' being Stub Wood.

A document of 1781 presents a rather different picture. In that year, Richard Thompson sold to one Samuel Wormald the Younger of the City of York, Woodmonger, no less than 850 oak trees on the Acaster Malbis estate. These came not from Stub Wood, but were 'now standing, growing and being within the Lordship of Acaster Malbis ... in the hedgerows thereof'. The trees were to be marked with a 'Number I' using a 'source iron'. Wormald paid a total of £1050, a large sum, 'To have hold cut down take and carry away all and singular the said several trees'.

The Indenture included various conditions about not causing damage on the estate, not least that they were to use the normal 'pathways' and 'gateways' for access and that they were to prevent damage to other trees during felling. They were also granted permission to make charcoal on waste land in the village and for that purpose 'to make Pitts and get sods and Dust', although Richard retained the right to say where such sods could be cut. The tenants were allowed to take stakes to repair any damaged fences until 1 May 1783.

The woodland may well be the reason why the Thompsons and their friends used to come over the river to hunt, a practise which had perhaps persisted for several hundred years. A gold signet ring found during ploughing in 1775 at the southern end of the parish had a Fleur de Lys and the initials B P, almost certainly Brian Palmes of Naburn who died in 1511.

PLACE-NAMES

In most villages, the best source of local place-names is the Tithe Award of the mid 1800s. Unfortunately, no such map exists for Acaster Malbis (see p 46) so we do not have a full list of field names. We do however have several medieval documents which refer to fields and streets, and quite a strong local oral tradition.

Documents from the thirteenth and fourteenth centuries give us some very interesting names, but the majority have been lost and we can only guess at their location. Amongst these names are Gevemersc, Dousgayle (geil = narrow lane), Landmerflat (mer = boundary), Lidgate (hlid-geat = 'swing-gate') and Lumbygayle (Lumby is probably a surname, with geil). Some names offer more clues as to their location: le Kirkeyat = church street; Lin(e)landes = flax lands – probably on the Ings. Two notable names found in thirteenth-century documents survive today – Stub Wood (1226) and Thomas Dyke (1277).

The last 150 years have also seen the loss of more recent names; Fred Raimes was busy recording lost names from elderly residents in the early 1900s. Amongst such names are 'Hods' ('strongholds'), small fields adjacent to the Ings into which the animals were driven at night. Gallowfield or Far Gallow Field lay near the Acaster/ Bishopthorpe boundary, the gate near the railway bridge being known as the Gallowgate. William Forth, an old Acastrian c 1900, spoke of Gallow Hill, which was destroyed by the railway. On the Appleton Road is Liberty Corner, marked by a small clump of trees and a bend in the road. This marked the point at which the Archbishop's Waste ended and Acaster Moor began (hence the name Moor End). Between the river and Moor End ran Ned Lane, stopped up in the late 1830s/early 1840s (see p 27).

The dyke names are some of the most long-lived; in addition to Thomas Dyke, we have Spah Dyke and Ciss Dyke to either side of The Green (the land north of the Ship Inn car park), Dimple Ditch and Scaffold Dyke. In the early nineteenth century the dykes near the Ship Inn were so foul that an outbreak of cholera was blamed on them. The villagers then decided to improve them, George Etherington planting a number of willow trees. The name 'Willow Garth' appears on Cooper's map of 1832.

The so-called 'Bakhus (or 'Baccus') Hill', halfway down Mill Lane, takes its name from a bakehouse which once stood there; the village stocks are also said to have stood near here. Cobbler's Trod, the original village street but now a footpath along the river bank, takes its name from the cobbler's shop which once stood in the grounds of what is now Richanchor. Intake Lane refers to land that has been 'taken in', ie enclosed.

Names like Mill Lane are fairly self-explanatory but there are red-herrings – Hauling (or Hawling) Lane probably has nothing to do with boats but takes its name instead from the hall which once stood behind the Ship Inn (see p 27).

Two notable Acaster families have their names immortalised in lane names: the Cowpers and the Darlings. Cowper Lane runs from Four Lanes End (cross-roads) to Moor End, ending at the corner adjacent to Dimple Cottage. Continuing on from the corner of Cowper Lane runs Darling Lane, along past the White Cottage T-junction before winding itself to an end back at the Appleton Roebuck road.

8
A Time of Change

From the eighteenth century onwards the quality and extent of written documents concerning the village improves. The benefits of educating the people and the increasing need and ability to record and formalise arrangements have provided a legacy of invaluable information.

The River

The river must always have played a key role in the life of Acaster Malbis, although there are few if any references to it in historical documents. From the time of the arrival of the Romans in York in the late first century AD, until the mid twentieth century, the city was a thriving port. When you remember that all these boats passed Acaster on their journey to and from the city, you start to realise how busy the river was, particularly at certain times dependent on the tide. The footpath along the river bank was originally a towpath for the bargemen, who called at the Fisherman's Arms or the Ship for refreshment.

The River Ouse was at one time tidal as far as Boroughbridge but by the mid eighteenth century, navigation was becoming increasingly difficult for larger vessels. After several surveys, it was decided to build a lock and dam at Naburn Ings in order to raise the water level in York by about five feet and thereby improve navigation. A leading campaigner for the dam was Richard Thompson, who was later to inherit the Acaster estate. The lock opened in 1757, having cost c £10,000, but unfortunately poor dredging downstream meant that many boats couldn't even reach the lock. In 1887 York Corporation decided to build a second, larger lock parallel to the first to enable steamers of up to 400 tons burden to reach the city. A tender of £8614 5s 8d from Messrs Nelson was accepted and the new lock was opened on 27 July 1889 by HRH Prince Albert Victor of Wales KG, who was serving with the 10th Royal Hussars, stationed in York.

The close proximity of the villages of Acaster Malbis and Naburn, including sharing the same church until the late nineteenth century, means that the villagers have long enjoyed close relations. The two villages were linked for several hundred years by a ferry, which only ceased to operate in the mid twentieth century. Church Ings are still sometimes referred to as the Ferry Fields as it was from down here that the cross-river ferry from Naburn operated between the two slipways. This ferry service had at one time been worked from outside the Ship Inn, directly across the river, but was moved to the centre of Naburn village in around 1825. It is thought this move came about because the main thoroughfare for the ferry traffic in Naburn went past Naburn Hall, home of the Palmes family, who found the intrusion to be a nuisance. There were in fact two ferries running from Naburn, a small rowing boat for foot passengers and a larger pontoon-type vessel for transporting horses and carts and animals (including the York and Ainsty Hunt). At the time of the Great Sale in 1898 (see p 56), a small parcel of land was retained by Lord Wenlock for the purposes of the ferry service. As can be seen in the

Figure 13 Naburn Lock full of barges, and the York Corporation Steam Tug, early 1900s.

Figure 14 The York and Ainsty Hunt crossing the river on the ferry, c 1932. (Note the wind pump on the Acaster bank.)

photograph the ferry was attached to a long chain running between the two banks of the river and was winched across by the ferryman turning on a large wheel. It is said that the ferry was summoned from the Acaster side by banging a tin tray with a rusty spanner left by the slipway! The large ferry service ceased to operate in 1947 after a major flood left the ferry boat high and dry in the middle of Naburn High Street! The small rowing boat carried on until the mid 1950s.

The wheel and chain device which operated the larger ferry superceded an earlier, less reliable system. The new apparatus was designed by two men who knew the pitfalls of the original system – James Lindley, the local blacksmith, and Joseph Reader, the ferryman and also a blacksmith. Lindley appears to have been a real 'ideas' man, having previously taken out a patent for an improved horseshoe.

Fishing

The River Ouse at Acaster Malbis is known today for its recreational coarse fishing, but from early times fishing was an important provider of food and employment, many villagers being both farmer and fisherman. Fishing has also been responsible for the demise of the unfortunate or unwary, as is evidenced in a letter written on 5 November 1555 by the Lord Mayor and Aldermen of York to Members of Parliament in London regarding the appointment of one Thomas Standeven to sit as coroner in connection with the drowning of Robert Hodgeson of Acaster

Malbysshe, fyssher, who died at Easter of the same year.

Commercial fishing for salmon (February to August), smelt (March to May) and lamprey (October to February) was carried out on the river until relatively recently, although none of these are a commercial proposition today. Now only a few licences for trapping eels are issued. The present salmon pass was built in the mid 1930s at the instigation of Lord Bolton to encourage salmon to spawn in the upper reaches of the River Ure.

By the eighteenth century the village was a fishing station, the Lord of the Manor leasing the fishing rights to the villagers. Fish such as salmon were caught in traps and then taken by the women to York market. In 1744 an agreement was drawn up between Lord Fairfax and the York Corporation listing the seven places within the manor where nets could be landed. These fishing points were listed as: The Hole; Acaster Ferry; High Dykes; The Cleake; Muck Middings; Low Board; Thompson.

Prior to the first Naburn lock and the weir being built in 1757 salmon were caught by the use of fish garths which consisted of a net attached to stakes placed in the river bed; the fish were then caught in the nets as the tide came in. After this date salmon continued to be caught below the weir by the use of drift nets which involved one person in a small boat and another person on the river bank; a net was paid-out from the boat in a large circle and fish were caught in the net as it was pulled in towards the bank.

Fishing lodges built from timber or brick were erected by some farmers and the remains of the sturdier brick buildings could still be seen up to the 1960s. One was situated on South Ings about 200 yards below the weir and another opposite Moreby Hall. The lodges were used as shelters by fishermen (and the occasional farm worker!) as well as for the obvious use of storing salmon and fishing tackle.

In 1803 there was uproar amongst the landowners and fishermen along the Ouse when York Corporation attempted to claim all the fishing rights between the city and 'Wharf's Mouth'. Such rights were a valuable commodity – in 1744 one Thomas Fireman was paying rent of eighteen guineas a year for those in Acaster. The dispute was to rumble on for 23 years, until in 1826 a committee was appointed to research the Corporation's claim and 'to come to an amicable adjustment of the dispute with Mr Lawley, Mr Thompson and other proprietors of land adjoining the river'. At one stage a committee was appointed to search the York Corporation Minute Books looking for documents to support their claim.

The dispute was clearly resolved in favour of the landowners since those Rights previously held by Lord Wenlock passed into the possession of the various farmers who bought strips of land on the Ings when the estate was sold in 1898. Mr Palmes of Naburn Hall owned the Rights on the Naburn bank. The two banks of the river were fished separately by James Leaf of Naburn (whose family held the netting rights for over 250 years) and by Francis and Tom Smith of Acaster. In the early 1900s James Leaf and Tom Smith went into partnership and they then fished the full breadth of the river together. The last fishing licence held by the Leaf/ Smith partnership was issued in February 1940 in the names of Francis Turton Smith, James Leaf, Ernest and Harold Smith; Harold, the sole survivor, still resides in the village today. The last licence holder was J Fairburn of Poplar Farm. Although

Figure 15 (above) Tom Smith and his son Francis Turton (Tot) fishing for salmon below the weir in 1905.
Figure 16 (below) Wicker lamprey trap and holding box.

Figure 17 The white whale shot by Tom Smith in 1905.

fishermen have been known to exaggerate, we can record on good authority that Ernest Smith often told of an almost unbelievable catch – 141 salmon caught before lunch one Sunday!

Before the First World War a lamprey race (now gone) was built at the Acaster side of the weir. Lamprey, tube-shaped fish which attach themselves to stones, are known to prefer clean water, which indicates the state of the Ouse at that time, and have for centuries been regarded as a delicacy. (Henry VIII's gout is said to have been brought about by a surfeit of lampreys.) The fish were caught in a wicker basket which was placed at the downstream end of the race. At one time Tom Smith used to send live lamprey by the thousand to Holland. He would pick them out of the trap by night and pack them into boxes under the light of an oil lamp. They would then be loaded at Naburn station onto the midnight train to Hull or Goole before being exported for fishing bait. At one time it was common after the river had been in flood for lampreys to be found stranded on South Ings downstream of the weir but they are now almost non-existent in the Ouse.

The Ouse is tidal as far as the weir and fish (and mammals) normally associated with the sea occasionally find their way inland as far as Acaster Malbis, only to be barred by the weir and locks. Several porpoises were caught in the salmon nets in the 1900s and in 1905 Tom Smith shot a white whale below the weir. The whale was subsequently hauled from the river downstream at Cawood before being displayed in York until it rotted. Its remains are now in the Yorkshire Museum in York.

The number of fish in the river declined rapidly after the war as a result of pollution but the efforts to clean up the Ouse over recent years are now bringing dividends, as is evidenced by news recently announced that there is now a greater head of salmon present than there has been for the last sixty years.

Whilst fishing as a necessity and a commercial proposition is now almost a thing of the past, angling for pleasure has become a very popular pastime. With the exception of stretches which remain in private hands, most of the fishing rights are currently leased by York Amalgamation of Anglers.

The Press Gang

The importance of fishing in the village had an unfortunate consequence: the Press Gang thought that the fishermen would make good sailors. During the eighteenth century, York, then a thriving port, received frequent visits from the notorious Press Gang, looking for sailors for the King's ships. One day, Jane Etherington overheard near Ouse Bridge that the Press Gang was coming to Acaster. She promptly dropped the panniers of fish from her horse and galloped bareback to the village to raise the alarm. By the time the Gang arrived, every able-bodied man had fled into the woods. In their fury the Press Gang trashed the standing corn and fired shots into the trees. Jane was, needless to say, the village heroine.

On another occasion it is said that her brother and a fellow villager found themselves surrounded by the Gang in a fishing lodge on the Ings. The men asked if they could change their heavy clothes and boots. Having done so, they then watched for an opportunity and ran for it across South Ings, jumping the Thomas Dyke, with the sailors in hot pursuit. It soon became dark and with their local knowledge the two men escaped. They then hid in the trees and at first light crossed the river to Bell Hall at Naburn where the Squire then put them into livery for the day; the law at that time said that a livery servant could not be pressed into the King's service.

Mills

Windmills were once a common site in the countryside, when every village had its own mill and miller and farmers took their corn to be ground into flour. The earliest record of a mill at Acaster Malbis is the 1763 map, which shows a fine post mill at the north end of the village, in a field to the west of Acaster Lane, between the church and Bridge Farm (see Fig 12 on p 29). The field retained the name Mill Hill Field into the twentieth century. A rural village like Acaster however would almost certainly have had a mill from medieval times. A post mill had a very large central post around which the whole structure was rotated in order to catch the wind.

This mill must have survived into the early nineteenth century as c 1900 George Etherington remembered that 'a man named John Croft lived in Acaster Mill when it was in the field near the church – it also belonged to him when it was removed'. At one time it was managed by a Robert Markham on behalf of his sister, whose husband had died.

Sometime in the early 1800s the decision was made to move the windmill to a site at the south end of what is now Mill Lane, opposite the end of the slipway, a site held in 1763 by Richard Kettlewell. As George Etherington describes the original mill as being 'removed', it may have been dismantled and rebuilt on the new site, a new windmill being expensive to build. The old site was perhaps considered rather inconvenient now that the main street had moved back from the river.

The Holmes family had the windmill for most of the nineteenth century. Thomas and Elizabeth and their three sons lived in the cottage opposite the mill, on the riverside. Thomas paid a yearly rent of £32 for the cottage and 'Mill Garth'. The miller did a good trade in the early years, but by the time their youngest son Richard took on the mill in 1875 there was scarcely enough trade to pay the rent, and in 1880 the windmill fell down. The historian William Camidge described it thus:

> One summer afternoon, when the wind had ceased its sighing and the sun displayed its quiet brilliancy – when all was still as the grave – the mill slid down in ruins. There was no apparent cause for the event; without a note of warning, and with very little noise, it fell, as if its cohesive powers had suddenly passed away.

After the mill's demise Richard Holmes continued as a flour dealer and joiner until his death in 1905. Many years ago a villager, Ernest Smith, remembered as a child being given $1\frac{1}{2}$d (less than 1p) by his mother and sent to Mr Holmes for a large bag of flour. The cottage later became the village post office.

The construction of the lock and dam at Naburn Ings in 1757 created an island in the river. This was ideally placed for a tide mill and on 1 May 1813 an

Figure 18 Richard Holmes outside Mill Cottage, c 1898.

Indenture was drawn up between George Palmes of Naburn (the landowner), and Joseph Smith and Robert Jones, both of Tadcaster. Palmes leased 'All that piece or parcel of land ... in the Townships of Naburn and Acaster Malbis in the County of York [comprising of] one acre and twenty-eight perches ... known by the name of the "Island"'. The lease, which was for 60 years, goes on to state that before 6 April 1820 they must spend not less than £3000 in erecting 'in a good substantial and workmanlike manner' one Water Mill with 'all such Machinery Works and conveniences as shall be proper and necessary', and complete a wharf for the loading and unloading of goods to and from the said mill; also cottages as necessary, and to employ not more than six people. They were not allowed to take on apprentices who would thereby gain a legal right of settlement in the village and could thus become a burden on the parish. The three-storey mill was built, together with living accommodation for the tenant, and operated as a corn mill until 1860. One enterprising tenant during this period, a Mr Parkin, persuaded the local magistrates that visiting workers required refreshment, and so for a few years there was a public house on the island.

In 1860, a Mr Jackson of the Fleet Mills in Leeds took over the tenancy and at great cost adapted the machinery to grind flint and Cornish stone. The powder from this process was shipped by canal to Castleford, where it was used for glazing pottery. The transport costs meant the project was not viable and it was abandoned a few years later.

A Mr Dobby then converted the mill back, and it operated as a successful corn mill until 1877. On 21 June of that year, while repairs were being carried out, the

Figure 19 Mill Cottage today (1999).

Figure 20 Naburn Mill, early C20.

mill caught fire. A messenger on horseback went to Fulford where a detachment of Scots Greys turned out, with a manual military fire engine. Unfortunately they got lost, but meanwhile the messenger had reached York and the York Corporation steam fire engine, drawn by four horses, turned out. By the time they arrived however the mill was a ruin, despite being surrounded by water! The mill was insured by the Yorkshire Insurance Co and was subsequently rebuilt. In 1913 the wheel was replaced by a turbine and it continued to operate until the 1950s, being finally demolished in 1958.

The Pinfold

One feature of village life administered originally by the Court Leet and later the Jury, was the Pinfold. The Pinfold is the small brick-built enclosure situated at the junction of Mill Lane and Hauling Lane. These structures, once a common feature in many English villages, were used for the temporary confinement of stray farm animals and only after the payment of a fine could the owners retrieve their 'lost' animals. Although it may appear a little severe to fine the owners for their errant beasts it was really in everyone's interests to have a deterrent, especially when the open-field system was in operation, as a loose animal could have caused much damage to many people's crops. The responsibility of the Pinfold was usually that of the Pinder and any fines would have been paid to the Lord of the Manor. Unfortunately we don't know the date of our Pinfold; the present structure probably dates from the eighteenth century but it almost certainly replaced a structure built of less durable materials.

It is not known when the Pinfold was last used in earnest but it was almost certainly in operation during the last century as the Court Leet records show that a new gate costing 3/6d was purchased for it in 1836. The 1846 List of Pains (see below) notes that 'all pigs found straying in the Common Lane or trespassing on Another Person's premises shall be impounded [presumably in the pinfold] and pay the usual forfeit'. The Pinfold is no longer a necessity today, although one or two trampled garden owners may dispute this, yet it stands in good condition thanks in part to repairs undertaken during the 1950s after a collision with a farm trailer and renovation work carried out in 1987.

In Acaster Malbis many of the medieval traditions continued well into the post-medieval period, some even surviving today. The Court Leet continued in the form of a township jury, which formulated a list of 'Pains' that had to be adhered to. This local court had the power to impose quite heavy fines.

The Memorandum of Pains laid on 13 November 1846 included:

We lay in Pain that every person mows his respective Portion of Meadow in the South Ings on or before the 12th day of July next; for each Default to lose his Fog*.

We lay in Pain that no persons shall have any Cattle in the Common Lanes before 6 o'clock in the Morning, nor after 8 o'clock in the Evening; for each Offence 5/- forfeit.

We lay in Pain that no Person shall cut any Grass or Reeds in the South Ings before the 1st day of July next; for each Offence 10/6 forfeit.

We lay in Pain that no Person shall make any Bon-fires within a quarter of a Mile of any Stack or the Town; for each Offence 10/6.

We lay in Pain that every Person shall clean and scour his respective Portion of Ditch from Abbey's Bridge to the River Ouse; for every Road undone One shilling forfeit.

[*Fog is a term used to describe the grazing rights on the Ings after the hay crop has been cut.]

A total of 24 Pains are listed, followed by a list of Jurymen.

The annual expenses from these records also highlight some other interesting points from the past. Throughout the 1800s a molecatcher was employed by the parish for which he was paid around £5 for his efforts; the costs for sparrow trapping ran to a similar amount, as large numbers of these birds could decimate a field of corn in a short space of time.

The Ship Inn

My Honest Friend,
I Tell You True,
Good Ale's Sold Here
By Mickey Drew

This handsome advertisement once adorned the sign for the Ship Inn and was the work of a slightly eccentric landlord called, not surprisingly, Michael Drew. He occupied the premises in the early 1800s and was well known for his love of reading. This literary man had the 'novel' idea of placing half of an old boat on end in the garden to form a study to which he frequently retreated to indulge his love of books. It was known locally as 'Mickey's cave'.

The Ship Inn stands on the site of the stables for the original manor house or hall which faced onto Hauling Lane (see p 27). It is not known whether these were of brick or timber but since the original part of the pub, the section built of the smaller bricks, may date from the late 1600s, it may incorporate part of the fabric of the stables. The bulk of the building however dates from the mid eighteenth century but it has been extended on several occasions since to meet the growing demands of trade. Like the neighbouring Blacksmith's Cottage, the older part of the building has Yorkshire sliding sashes.

The Ship Inn has a long history of providing refreshment for passing trade as well as locals, most notably the Ouse bargemen who found it a welcome port of call after an arduous haul up the river. When coming up stream the barges travelled along the South Ings to just below the weir and then crossed over to the Naburn

Acaster

Figure 21 Postcard of the Ship Inn and Blacksmith's Cottage, c 1925

side to gain access through the lock. They then travelled on the other side of the river up to the crossing point, which was located at the entrance to the Church Ings and fortunately just a short walk from the Inn. It is said that they received their refreshing tankards of ale from a small serving hatch, which can still be seen in the wall to the left of the fireplace, and were discouraged from coming in to the pub due to their irregular hygiene habits.

Many of the bargemen would have smoked a clay pipe, and a large collection has been recovered from fields near the river. Tobacco and clay tobacco pipes were introduced to this country in the late sixteenth century. By the seventeenth century tobacco was being grown in England, including the Vale of York, and pipe manufacturers had sprung up all over the country. The pipes from Acaster include some very early examples, from c 1610 to 1630, while others from c 1660 to 1680 can be attributed to Abraham Boyes of York and Robert Burril of Hull, their initials being stamped on the base. Not surprisingly, the pipes reflect the trading links between York and Hull. White pipe clay was also used to produce hair curlers in the late seventeenth and eighteenth centuries and several of these have also been found. They presumably belonged to the more permanent residents of the village!

Correspondence in the church archives reveals that there was considerable opposition to the granting of a seven-day licence to the Ship Inn in the 1890s. One objector declared that 'undesirable women would come out from York in charabancs'.

Unfortunately for the pub's patrons and especially the landlord, being in such close proximity to the river predisposes the Ship Inn, and a few other properties, to occasional flooding. This may cause a headache for the landlord but perhaps the absence of one for his regulars. In March 1947 the York area experienced one of the worst floods within living memory with many properties being flooded, the Ship Inn being no exception. The waters managed to enter the oven at the side of the fireplace and as reported by one determined individual, 'The water came up to the money in my back pocket'. The pub used to have a traditional cellar which of course flooded, so this was filled in prior to the building of an extension in 1966.

The pub, like most properties in Acaster, moved into private hands when the Acaster Estate was sold in 1898 and ownership was transferred from Lord Wenlock to Robert Couch Kent, who lived in Acomb. The sale price of £1650 included The Green, which is now the river frontage of Poplar Farm, and a small orchard behind the pub which has since disappeared. This orchard was almost certainly part of the original hall grounds. The landlord at the time was Frederick Tyler, whose name appears on the Acaster Roll of Honour (see p 62).

The landlord of the Ship Inn today still trades in 'good ale' and it is still a popular calling point for the boating fraternity, although the river traffic is now entirely pleasure boats, a far cry from even fifty years ago. The caravan sites also bring good business to the pub in the summer months.

The Ship Inn was not the only pub in the village in the mid nineteenth century. The house now known as the Old Vicarage (see p 10) opened as a public house, the appropriately named Fisherman's Arms, in 1842. The building, which had been declared 'unfit for residence' in 1818, was enlarged by the tenant landlord, Samuel Darling and his wife Sarah, at their own expense. Upstairs, a wooden partition could be removed to make one large room and for several years the Court Leet dinners given by Lord Wenlock were held there. A Trade Directory of 1857 lists the tenant as John Darling, tailor and victualler, and his wife Ann. Sadly the inn closed soon after 'for want of trade', the Ship Inn by this time being the prime village hostelry. The building then became the village shop run by Ann Darling (see Fig 8 on p 10), the great-grandmother of the later post-mistress Mabel Stott.

POPULATION

As population surveys were not introduced in England until the 1800s, the first national census being taken in 1801, it is very difficult to state with any accuracy the number of people who resided in Acaster Malbis at any given period before that. At various times however taxes were levied nationally which give some indication of the number of dwellings in the parish and its population.

The first national survey of England was the Domesday Book of 1086, although it is not always very easy to understand: Acaster Malbis had three villagers with two ploughs while Copmanthorpe had three villagers and two smallholders with only one plough!

Fortunately, later taxes are a little easier to interpret and the Poll Taxes raised in the fourteenth, seventeenth and eighteenth centuries provide a much better insight into the make-up of the village. The first Poll, or head tax was levied in 1377, on those over fourteen years of age. The returns for the West Riding of the Poll Tax laid in the second year of the reign of Richard II (1379) show that Nobles and Archbishops had to pay £6 13s 4d, Merchants 1s, Tradesmen or Handicraftmen 6d and Labourers a groat (4d). The 1379 Tax was levied on those aged over sixteen. Records show that in 'Acaster Malbysshe' a total of 44 villagers were taxed; 43 paid 4d and one person, Johannes de Kyrkby, a textor (a weaver or worker in textile fabrics) paid 6d. Acaster was clearly not a wealthy parish in the late fourteenth century.

It is interesting to note that of the 37 males taxed, sixteen had the name of Johannes and eight were called Willelmus; of the seven females taxed, four were named Alicia. There seems to have been a serious lack of imagination in the choice of christian names at this time amongst both the poor and the wealthy!

It is more difficult to account for the gross imbalance between males and females; certainly there is some evidence for a shorter life expectancy for females in the medieval period but a ratio of only 1:7 seems exceptional. Perhaps the figure is distorted by a large number of farm labourers in the village.

The Hearth Tax was introduced soon after the Restoration in 1660, with the intention of providing an adequate income for Charles II. The Tax was applied to the occupiers of property worth twenty shillings or more and the rate charged was two shillings per hearth, paid equally at Lady Day and Michaelmas. It included forges, mills and common ovens but exempted property owned by the church or charities and industrial hearths. Lists survive for most years between 1662 and 1674; on Lady Day 1672 the Hearth Tax was levied on 40 people in 'Acaster Maulbiey'. The total population of the parish at that time is not known but the list provides a good indication of the size of the village. It must be remembered that only properties worth twenty shillings or more were included.

The nearby village of Askham Richard is shown to have a smithy, while Bilbrough had a forge; there is no record of Acaster Malbis having either, although a smithy existed until only a few years ago. Perhaps the property was not worth twenty shillings.

The village had clearly expanded considerably in the three hundred years since the Poll Tax of 1379. Amongst the family names are those of Doubty (later Doughty) and Darling, names which occur frequently in village records from the seventeenth century onwards (Appendix 1). Indeed, the Darling family gave its name to a lane in the village!

Two documents from the Wenlock archives give some clues as to the size of the village in the eighteenth century. Firstly, the estate map of 1763 has a list of all the tenants, a good indication of the number of households. A total of 46 names appear, suggesting the village had not changed much in the preceding hundred years.

The second document relates to the Land Tax levied by the government in 1798. Each farm was valued and a tax levied according to acreage, to be paid annually from 25 March 1798. The annual tax for Acaster Malbis was put at £165 8s 5d on an estate of 1771 acres of land, a fishery in the River Ouse 'with the Dwellinghouses and other Buildings erected in the said Estate'. As landlord, Richard Thompson was liable for the tax and documents reveal that he elected to redeem the tax 'in perpetuity' by one payment. The redemption value was put at £6317 13s 4d, a large sum in the late eighteenth century, and provision was made for payment in instalments. Thompson however chose to pay one lump sum in May 1799 and the tax was duly registered 1 June 1799. A total of 35 farms are listed, paying sums ranging from as little as 3s 1d to £23 19s 1d (Appendix 1). Allowing for the estate map being a list of tenants rather than farms, the numbers are broadly compatible. Once more several members of the Darling family are listed, and names familiar to the present day such as Raimes and Cundall make their first appearance.

By the early nineteenth century government bureaucracy was increasing rapidly and accurate figures for population are much easier to come by. Census figures are available every ten years from 1801 onwards and these show a population for the village generally in the range 250 to 300, reaching a peak in 1841 of 322, but dropping back to only 231 ten years later. In 1901 the figure was only 227, which probably reflects the agricultural depression of the late 1800s.

One source of information from the nineteenth century that is missing for Acaster Malbis is a Tithe Award. Tithes were a tenth of the annual income from the land that was payable to the church or clergy. Tithes were originally paid in kind, hence the term 'tithe barn', but in the post-medieval period they were increasingly paid in money. After the Dissolution of the Monasteries by Henry VIII in the 1530s, the tithe became payable to the Crown. In the 1850s the government decided to record in detail land ownership and the amounts payable, ordering Tithe Awards to be made. These included a map and a list of all the owners and tenants. They are usually an important source of evidence for the history of any village.

As with the Land Tax, the landowner was ultimately responsible and once again the Wenlock estate decided to pay a lump sum to 'commute' the tithes once and for all. Thus although we have a document recording the commutation, we don't have a Tithe Award.

Another useful source of information in the second half of the nineteenth century are the local trade Directories. These were an early form of advertising but also included interesting pen sketches of villages and towns. The York and District Directory for November 1898 puts the population at about 250 and lists various parishioners and their occupations (Appendix 1).

The Electoral Roll for 1998 records 426 adults in the parish, 74 of whom lived at Lakeside and 47 at Mount Pleasant.

9

To School and Chapel

L ife in small villages since the nineteenth century has often revolved around institutions such as the church, the pub, the school and the village post office/shop. At one time Acaster Malbis could boast all four of these features, but sadly both the school and the post office have now closed.

The Methodist Chapel

> Another instance of the progress and vitality of Wesleyan Methodism in York and neighbourhood was furnished yesterday in the laying of Memorial Stones of a new chapel now in the course of erection of that denomination in Acaster Malbis.

Thus the *York Herald* for Friday 23 April 1880 described the foundation of the Methodist Chapel in Mill Lane. Methodism had in fact existed in Acaster Malbis for over a hundred years, and was very strong in the village. Tradition tells that John Wesley himself once preached a sermon in Acaster Malbis, taking the text 'Can any good come out of Nazareth?' as his theme. He commenced his discourse by saying 'Can any good come out of Acaster?'! The sermon is thought to have taken place in the front room of Richard Holmes' house – Mill Cottage – which was a regular meeting place. The first Methodist sermon preached in the village is said to have been delivered in the dining room of Mr Raimes' house (now Manor Guest House). The annual missionary meetings seem to have been very festive occasions; proceedings commenced with tea, then the actual meeting was held in a large barn at Mr Cundall's (Mount Pleasant), followed by lavish suppers at all the farms.

Lord Wenlock very generously donated a plot of land for the new chapel and the money to build it was raised by public subscription, with the benefactors having their names engraved on the memorial stones. Amongst the list of subscribers were John Raimes, R H Cundall and Robert Cowper, all Methodists at that time. What is interesting is how many non-Methodists made donations, including Mr H F Cundall of Hall Garth, who was a churchwarden at Holy Trinity, and Mr Poad of Beechlands, another 'church' regular. Priory Street Chapel in York also made a donation. The whole enterprise seems to have been a fine example of ecumenical endeavour and the original subscribers would no doubt be pleased to

Figure 22 Sketch of the Wesleyan Chapel published in the York Herald *at the time of its opening on 16 October 1880.*

know that church and chapel worship together once a month and support each other.

The foundation ceremony opened with 'the singing of the well-known hymn "This stone to thee we lay in faith", followed by an appropriate prayer'. The weather being 'very fine' according to the *Herald*, 'there was a numerous attendance of ladies and gentlemen present from York and the surrounding villages'.

The chapel site was well located near the centre of the village, on slightly rising ground. The chapel, in the Early English style, was designed by Mr C Anderson of Lendal, York, and the contractor was Mr John Simpson of Priory Street, York. It is built of Potternewton stone with Whitby stone dressings. The building measures *c* 55 feet by 23 feet and is capable of seating about 150 people. The original estimate for the building work was £1000, but it was completed for only £890 – less than was spent *restoring* Holy Trinity at about the same time.

The opening service took place on 16 October 1880 and was again attended by 'a large number of ladies and gentlemen from York', most of whom arrived on the steamer *White Rose*. The preacher was the Rev Sholl of Leeds, who also preached at the foundation ceremony. After the service 'an excellent tea' was provided in a barn at The Hollies, then the home of the Cowpers. The chapel continues in regular use although the seating capacity was perhaps always optimistic!

Acaster Malbis School

John Knowles in his will dated 18 August 1603 provided for the appointment of a schoolmaster for the village. Unfortunately, the trail then goes cold but it is assumed that his instructions were carried out, although the location of the schoolroom and the date when it was erected are not known. We do know that one of the nineteenth-century schoolmasters was called Mr Billy Lee and he and his wife were fondly remembered in the village *c* 1900. Mr Lee (who also doubled-up as post-master) was rather stout and the boys used to play tricks on him ... for which they duly suffered!

In 1906 the Parish Meeting claimed that in 1764 the inhabitants of Acaster Malbis purchased a Schoolhouse by voluntary contribution consisting of two rooms of one storey each covered by a thatched roof and lit by small leaded windows. The two rooms comprised the schoolmaster's residence and a teaching area. This was erected on land described as the Lord's Waste and is thought to have been not far from the river in the vicinity of Inglewood. A Charity Commission Report to Parliament dated 1895 suggests the purchase was made *c* 1778, but 1764 may well be correct. Where the school operated from in the seventeenth and early eighteenth century we do not know.

In 1876 the charity school was replaced by a mixed Public Elementary School. This opened its doors on 24 April 1876 under the Certified Mistress Elizabeth Healey, the average attendance at that time being 25. The school was housed in a single-storey building half way along Mill Lane, opposite the point known locally as the 'Baccus', or Bakehouse Hill. The building, still known as the School House, is now a private dwelling; an adjacent building provided accommodation for the schoolmaster.

On 18 May 1877 Elizabeth Healey resigned and was replaced on 31 May 1877 by Louisa Sophia Dobing. Only seventeen scholars were present: this may have been because the school presumably had been closed for two weeks in the absence of a teacher, although attendance normally fluctuated between 26 and 35 as several boys attended irregularly because they were required to work on the farms.

In the 1880s attendance during the summer and autumn months remained very poor as some pupils were still required to work in the fields. The School Inspector's Report of 11 May 1883 declares 'the School is improving under Mrs Whitaker especially in reading. The infants promises well.' These comments were made by Robert Cowper, a local man who must have been of some standing as his name is celebrated in one of the road names. He went on to say that 'the teacher is assisted by the more advanced scholars in the first class. Average attendance 40.9.' On 17 December 1886 Margaret Whitaker gave up charge of the school and was replaced by Clara Jane Adcock.

The turn-over of staff remained high; on 28 September 1891 William Hughes took charge. There is no record of him having left the school but by 4 January 1893 Mona B Wroe was in charge. She continued until at least 1899, when the School Register from which we have extracted this information comes to an end, at which time there were 40 pupils. Attendance figures of around 40 for much of

Figure 23 The assembled gathering at the burying of a time capsule beneath a horse chestnut tree outside the village school in 1908. (Note Fred Raimes in back row on right, with bowler hat, Tom Smith behind.)

Fig 24 The Class of 1930
Back row: Marcia Mothersill; Margery Wood; Hilda Brown; Christine Mothersill; Hilda Martindale. Middle row: Margery Brown; Gordon Waller; Norman Masterman; Thomas Atkinson; Norman Wood; Harold Smith; Geoffrey Smith; Lillian Wilson. Front row: Norman Taylor; Gladys Goodin; Fred Taylor; Joan Brown.

the late nineteenth century reflect a flourishing, well-populated village.

By 1908 a Miss Rothery was in charge and it was she who organised the planting of a horse chestnut tree outside the school, with a bottle containing the names of the pupils buried beneath it. The event was recorded in an early photograph. The tree is still standing and yields a good crop of conkers for today's children.

In 1920 Miss Reader took charge assisted by Miss Mabel Jackson as infant teacher. Miss Reader was very strict and had been brought in to calm the unruly element. Her daily expedition to and from school was testimony to her perseverance: she lived in Selby and each morning caught a train to Naburn Station; she then walked to the ferry and crossed the river before walking along the river bank to school. Pupils were no doubt pleased when the Ouse was in flood because the ferry was cancelled ... and so was school.

By 1930 pupil numbers were down to seventeen and in 1947 Acaster Malbis School finally closed and the pupils transferred to Bishopthorpe. Ironically, the development of the village in the last 30 years has meant that a large number of children now have to be transported to neighbouring villages to receive their primary education.

The Post Office

Post Office records show that the first 'Date Stamp' to be issued at Acaster Malbis was on 4 March 1839. At this time the post office operated from Cobbler's Cottage, in the garden of what is now Richanchor. Letters arrived daily at 9.30am by foot post from York. One of the first post-masters was William Lee, who was also the schoolmaster. In the early twentieth century the post office was operated by one Robert Cowper from the property now known as Inglewood, next door to the old school. Being the post-master was clearly not a full-time occupation, since Robert Cowper also worked as a joiner.

In 1932 Mabel Holmes married Ted Stott and moved into Mill Cottage, where her great-uncle Richard had been the miller until his death in 1905. Mill Cottage then became the post office and Mabel remained the post-mistress for over 40 years, finally retiring in 1976 when she handed over to her daughter Marian. Marian Shoobridge continued until her death in 1991, after which the post office and shop was run by her husband Stan and sister Vivienne. The post office finally closed in December 1993.

The Railway

On 2 January 1871 the railway finally came to Acaster Malbis, but it was of little use to the villagers since the nearest station was across the river at Naburn. The line passed through the northern tip of the parish, leaving a small parcel of land isolated to the north. This land, which was later used to build cottages for railway

Figure 25 The Flying Scotsman crossing Naburn Bridge in 1969.

workers, is still part of Acaster Malbis parish, the cottage residents being required to vote in Acaster, not Bishopthorpe.

The line, which ran between the junctions at Barlby North and Chaloner's Whin, was built by the North Eastern Railway to provide a direct route between Doncaster and York via Selby, replacing the earlier route via Knottingley and Church Fenton, and formed part of the East Coast Main Line between London and Scotland. Large expresses were thus a common sight.

The principal feature on this section of line was the bridge over the Ouse between Naburn and Acaster Malbis. The bridge, which still survives, consists of two spans, the northern of which rotated to allow the passage of tall river craft. The bridge was operated from a small cabin situated above the rotating span. The decline in river traffic led to the bridge being fixed in 1956, although the cabin remained in use as a signal box until 1967. The line was closed on 24 September 1983 and was replaced by a new railway between Colton Junction several miles to the west of Acaster Malbis, and Templehurst Junction south of Selby to allow the development of the Selby coalfield.

The old trackbed, including the bridge, is now a well-used cycle track between York and Selby.

Peppermint

Peppermint, pungent and a little sharp on the tongue, goes down well with a tot of rum but the watered-down version that we know today is totally different from the pure, hard peppermint that was the age-old brew. Neat peppermint is a volatile liquid which bears as close a resemblance to firewater as makes no difference.

Peppermint is brewed from the herb *Mentha Piperath* and the manufacture of peppermint was once a thriving cottage industry going back many generations. It is thought that it was cultivated in the Moor End part of Acaster Malbis and there is evidence that it was distilled in the village. It was used in its watered-down version to cure a variety of ailments, from the common cold to stomach-ache.

The only remaining relic of the industry in the village is the cast-iron object said to be part of a peppermint still in use around 1840 which now stands outside the Memorial Hall. The object received its proper recognition only after being used as a water butt in the cow byre at The Hollies farm before the buildings were converted to residential use. The still (water butt) came under the auctioneer's hammer at The Hollies farm sale conducted for retiring farmers Henry Wood & Sons in 1971 and was purchased for £10 by F G Smith, the then Chairman of the Acaster Malbis Parish Meeting. It was resited at its present location as a reminder of part of the village's heritage.

Government bureaucracy brought about the end of the cottage peppermint industry throughout the country. Distilled peppermint is a liquor, like whisky, and around the time of the First World War it was decided that in future licences would be required to operate stills. Rather than pay for something which for years had been their birthright, the cottage-based distillers objected in the strongest possible way – they smashed their stills and brought about the industry's decline.

BUILDINGS

Surprisingly for a village with such a long history, Acaster Malbis can boast only four Listed Buildings (ie buildings regarded as being of special architectural interest), and one of these is the church! (The others are Hall Garth, the Old Vicarage and the Ship Inn.) Like many lowland rural areas, timber would have been the principal building material, being cheap and readily available (see p 30); bricks were an expensive luxury that few could afford. The wholesale shift of the village street at the end of the eighteenth century is also no doubt partly to blame. At least one cottage on the river bank survived well into the twentieth century, towards the southern end of Mill Lane, and was recorded by Fred Raimes *c* 1900. Most of the older buildings date from the eighteenth century, but both Portland Cottage and Chestnut Farm have their origins in the later seventeenth century. Portland Cottage was originally a salmon smokehouse and at one time there was a petrol pump outside. The Listed Building description suggests that Hall Garth dates from the late seventeenth century on the basis of the roof timbers, but the 1763 estate map shows a building on Cobbler's Trod, facing the river. The present Hall Garth, in origin a farmhouse, probably dates to the late eighteenth century, being moved back from the river to avoid flooding and turned through 90° to a more favourable southerly aspect. The roof timbers of the original building may well have been recycled into the new farmhouse, being expensive commodities. The building was extended to the north in the nineteenth century, and again in the early twentieth century. As well as the dwelling house, Hall Garth also includes an extensive range of outbuildings, amongst which is a three-seater (two adults and a child) earth privy! (It is pleasing to note that Hall Garth has recently (1999) been sold and restoration work is about to begin.)

The early eighteenth century saw a major programme of building in the village: the Ship Inn and Blacksmith's Cottage date from the early 1700s, while the Old Vicarage (Fisherman's Arms) has a datestone of 1732. At the other end of the village, the old post office (Mill Cottage) was constructed c 1740 and Manor Farm and the original Southmoor House are from the early to mid 1700s. Beechlands Farm on the way to Appleton Roebuck is dated by a beam in the roof with the year 1785 inscribed upon it.

Dimple Cottage is a charming cottage that takes its name from the nearby Dimple Ditch. It appears to date from the early 1700s and has been extended several times over the years. The pitch of the roof indicates that it, like several other properties in the village, was originally thatched. The interior still retains a number of interesting features, including an upstairs fireplace and a panelled interior door complete with an ingenious casement lock. Outside there is probably the last surviving well in Acaster. In 1923 Charles Wilson, a widower and local bricklayer, bought the cottage and land from the council for £235 and moved in with his *eight* children. After his death in 1934 the eldest daughter, Emily, then aged fourteen, brought up her four sisters and three brothers. She continued to live at Dimple Cottage until her death in 1992.

From the nineteenth century, Poplar Farm stands out as the only three-storey building in the village. Virtually all the properties at Moor End date from the late nineteenth/early twentieth century, reflecting the reorganisation of that area since the 1763 estate map, although the earliest deed for Wenlock House (previously Warren House, previously Bramblewick) is dated 28 June 1839. Wenlock House appears to have been part of the marriage settlement between the third Baron Wenlock and his wife Lady Elizabeth Grosvenor, daughter of the Duke of Westminster. Sometime around 1858 one Joseph Johnson Leeman became the owner; the famous Lord Mayor, MP and Chairman of the North Eastern Railway George Leeman is known to have had relatives in Acaster so it is reasonable to assume the two were related. The twentieth century saw the demolition of several cottages, including the White Cottage, on a tiny parcel of land lying between Darling Lane and the Dimple Ditch, close to the corner of Mill Lane, and Godmother Row, three cottages that stood adjacent to York Cottage at Moor End.

10
A New Beginning

The Great Sale

The turn of the last century must have been a period of uncertainty for many in the village, for after over eight hundred years under a single landlord, in 1898 the Wenlocks put the Acaster Malbis Estate up for sale. At a time of agricultural depression, Lord Wenlock had decided to concentrate his estates on the east bank of the river. Several villagers bought their cottages and became landowners for the first time in their lives; for others there was a new landlord.

The estate was sold by Public Auction at the Station Hotel, York on Thursday 15 December 1898. It was described as comprising '9 farms, 27 Small Holdings, Cottages, and Gardens, and also that Licensed Public House known as The Ship Inn. Together with all the Manorial and Sporting Rights of the Property, and the Salmon fisheries in the River Ouse'.

Under 'General Remarks', the sale brochure notes that the rentals are low because of the depression, the total being £2733 10s 0d, not including the woodlands which were in hand. The land was described as 'Freehold, Tithe Free and Land Tax redeemed', the only charge being the £12 annual payment to the Vicar of Acaster, to be charged on Lot 9 (Acaster [now Garth] Farm). There were also two improvement rent charges of £54 5s 2d on the farm held by Messrs Poad (Beechlands), and £74 0s 10d on Raimes (Manor) Farm.

The Ship Inn raised £1650, being bought by Robert Couch Kent of Gale Lane, Acomb, while the publican, Frederick Tyler, bought Lots 18 and 20, the two fields either side of Hauling Lane.

A number of the large farms, including Acaster, The Hollies and Nova Scotia remained unsold, presumably because they did not meet their reserve price. It would seem these were sold by private treaty at a later date, as was Southmoor House, occupied by John and Isobel Raimes. John had inherited the tenancy of the House and farm in 1846, and the land had been farmed by their son William, who died shortly before the Sale. Another son, Fred, who had made his fortune as an industrialist on Teesside, then stepped in, purchasing not only Southmoor House and Manor Farm but also the Lordship and its rights.

Even prior to the Sale, Fred Raimes had been concerned to improve the property. On the occasion of Queen Victoria's Diamond Jubilee in 1897, he invited every

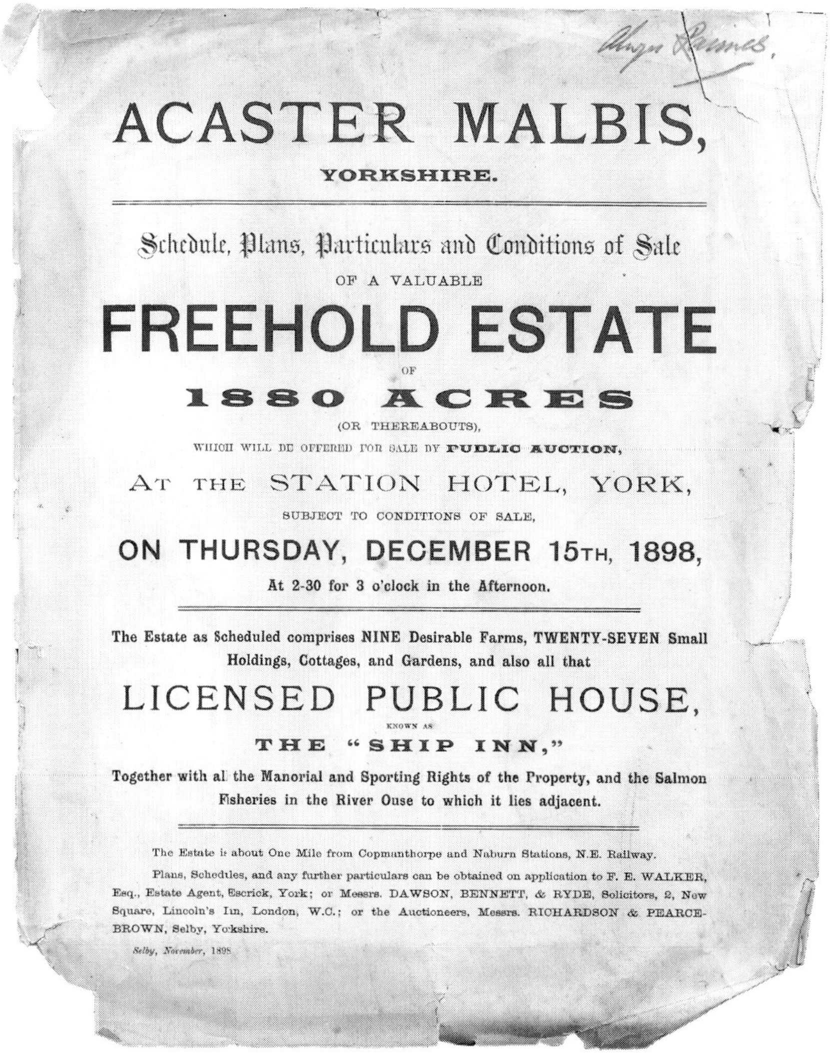

Figure 26 Extract from the Sale Particulars, 1898.

couple to a celebration at Southmoor with the instruction that the men were to bring spades! The reason became apparent later in the afternoon, when each couple was invited to plant a copper beech tree along the southern boundary of Southmoor's gardens. This curving line of magnificent copper beeches can still be seen today.

Following his purchase, Fred then set about turning Southmoor into a country gentleman's 'seat', refronting and extending the House, imparking *c* 120 acres (50ha), planting an avenue and clumps of trees in iron-railed enclosures and installing Highland Cattle. He also created a 5 acre (2ha) 'pleasure ground' to the east of the House, with a large lake and a folly in the form of part of the ruins of

57

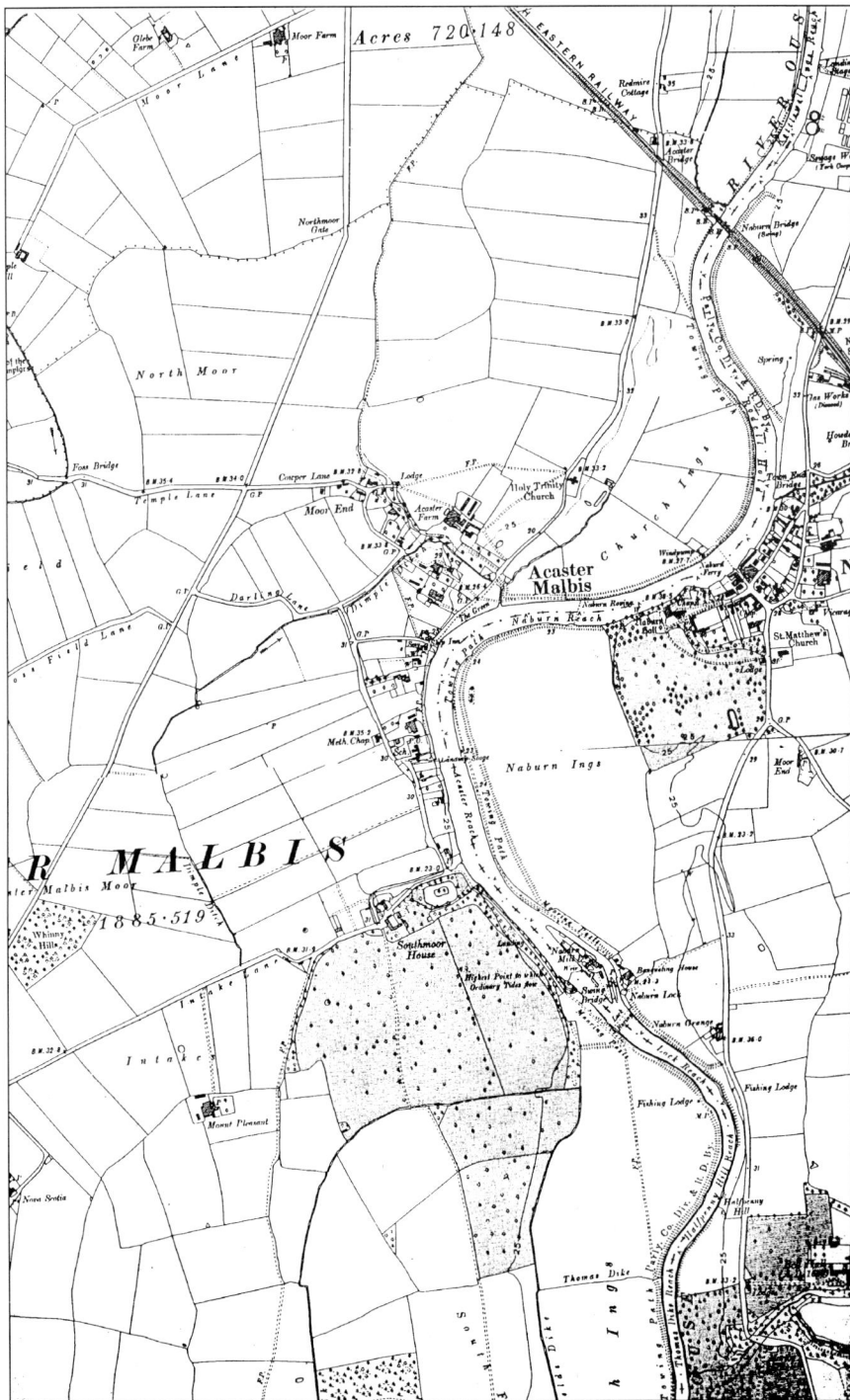

Figure 27 2nd edition OS map, revised 1906, published 1910.

St Andrew's church, Bishopthorpe.

The House was heavily modernised and its external appearance gives no clue as to its eighteenth-century origin. In particular, the Manor and its adjacent farmhouse had the luxury of flushing toilets while nearby greenhouses and animal troughs had never-ending supplies of water, thanks to an ingenious system of obtaining water from the river. A reciprocating ram (a type of pump operated by water pressure) was sited near the weir; water was then piped to a storage tank mounted above outbuildings at the Manor which was hidden behind castellated walls (now demolished) and drawn off as required. Surplus water found its way back into the river via a series of ponds in the Manor gardens. The ram system was disposed of several years ago when piped fresh water was brought to Acaster, but the ponds (with a water system served by an electric pump) happily still exist.

John Raimes died shortly after the Sale but Fred's mother and unmarried sisters continued to live there. The First World War brought about a downturn in Fred's fortunes, but the farm remains in the hands of the Raimes family today.

Southmoor House was let in 1947 as a private school and in 1960 it was sold to a Mr Harley Ebbs, remaining a school until *c* 1965. It then became the Manor Guest House, Manor Farm now being run from the farmhouse opposite.

Fred Raimes, perhaps mindful of his role as Lord of the Manor, seems to have spent some time recording the memories of the older villagers. His handwritten notes survive and have been used in the preparation of this book. His brother Herbert spent many hours researching the Raimes family history, and also that of Acaster Malbis; his notebook has proved an invaluable source of information.

Farming 1911-2000

The countryside as we see it today reflects the transformation that has taken place in almost every aspect of farming in the twentieth century. The farms in Acaster Malbis were mainly traditional mixed farms, with crops grown in a rotation to preserve fertility; fodder for cattle, sheep and pigs was grown as well as food crops.

In the early 1900s most of the people of the village were involved in working the land, like their fathers before them. Before the advent of mechanical power, horses played a key role in farming. Ploughing, cultivation, harvesting, haymaking and haulage all required genuine horse power. The village blacksmith was an essential member of the community and his shop was situated adjacent to the Ship Inn. The shop was operated by J Richardson & Son and they were kept busy shoeing horses, making new farm harrows and repairing farm equipment.

Steam-driven threshing machines and ploughing engines began to supplement horse power in this area in the early 1900s, a massive leap forward and it was not until after the Second World War that tractors began to replace horses and combine harvesters replaced the steam-driven threshing machines. At one time two steam threshing sets were operated within a six-mile radius of the village by J W Jefferson, who lived at Bramblewick (now Wenlock House), Moor End.

The small tractor such as that made by Ferguson revolutionised land work.

Figure 28 Steam thresher at Poplar Farm in the 1920s.

Over the years powerful machines such as the combine harvester, the four-wheel-drive tractor capable of pulling huge ploughs with ease, the root harvester and the baler have become standard equipment on arable farms. The use of such efficient machinery has speeded-up or totally removed much of the labour intensive, time-consuming and heavy work involved in many traditional farm processes. The endless drive to achieve efficiency and reduce costs has however had an adverse effect on the number of people actually employed on the farms; several farms have diverged away from farming completely whilst others supplement their income in other ways such as ice cream manufacture, stabling and animal feed retailing. The picturesque armies of stooked corn have been replaced by bales of hay, straw and silage in the now familiar round and rectangular shapes and even the vista has changed as new crops have introduced new colours, such as the yellow of oil seed rape and the blue of linseed.

It is neither desirable nor possible to turn the clock back to the era of unmodernised farming yet there was much to be valued in the old system of mixed husbandry of Acaster's family farms.

After the sale of the Acaster Malbis estate by Lord Wenlock in 1898 the farms were initially purchased by private owners. The Government however supported the breaking-up of large farms to enable the young men of the area to make a start in farming, and in 1911, Acaster Farm at Moor End became the first farm in the village to be bought by the West Riding County Council (WRYCC). This became four separate small-holdings: Garth Farm, Bridge Farm, Lodge Farm and Foss

Farm. In the case of Garth and Bridge Farms, the Earles and the Mastermans are only the second tenants since 1911. (All the farms previously owned by WRYCC have now been sold.)

The second large farm to be bought by the Council was Poplar Farm, owned by J Penty & Sons who moved to Bolton Percy. Again four small-holdings were created, as well as three new farm-holdings built in 1921 which were let to ex-servicemen. The farms created were: Poplar Farm (now a Caravan Park), Whitemoor Farm, Longfield Farm and Park Farm.

The last large farm to be purchased and split-up by the Council was Nova Scotia, which was bought from William Bellerby, a racehorse owner and trainer. This farm was tenanted for a short time by Sidney Atkinson but in 1930 he gave up farming to become the landlord of the Ship Inn. The tenancy was then taken by Henry Jackson & Son, who moved from Chestnut Farm. In 1936 four small-holdings were created: Poplar Grove, Westfield, Woodside and Nova Scotia. The latter was later taken over by the RAF and is now the site of the Waterline Leisure boatyard.

Shortly before the outbreak of war in 1939 the Council built their last small-holding, which they named Fossfield Farm. This was created from land previously tenanted by J H Fairburn of Poplar Farm. Fossfield Farm is now the home of the popular and delicious Yorvale real dairy ice cream.

St Andrew's (Tandrew's) Farm, and the neighbouring farm of the same name in Appleton Roebuck parish were taken over by the RAF to form the airfield.

Several privately owned farms still remained after the Second World War but the last 50 years have seen substantial changes. Chestnut Farm now operates solely as a seasonal Caravan Park, while Moor End Farm operates as both a farm and a caravan park. Much of Mount Pleasant Farm became a residential Caravan Park, with Intake Grange Farm formed from the remainder of the land. The Hollies on Mill Lane was broken up 40 years ago. Only Beechlands and Manor Farm still survive in something like their original form.

Robert Cooper's Map of the Ainsty in 1832 shows that Mount Pleasant Farm was previously known as Stubb Wood House, the name being changed sometime between then and 1846, when the OS 1st edition 6" map was surveyed, while it was the home of Mr and Mrs Robert Abbey. Mr and Mrs Abbey, 'Wesleyans of the old school', are said to have found the place very congenial to them, hence the name.

Acaster Memorial Hall

Acaster Memorial Hall was built in 1927 to commemorate the men of the village who fought in the First World War, six of whom were killed in action. The land was purchased from the then West Riding County Council for the particularly reasonable sum of £6 and was handed over to eight men from the village to oversee its construction.

The Hall's pedigree could not be more Acastrian: it was built using bricks manufactured at the old brickworks, now Lakeside, and constructed by local builder George Fairburn, his brother Herbert, a joiner, and Charles Wilson, a bricklayer, all of whom lived in the Moor End area. Even the total cost of £300, a considerable sum given the size of the village at the time, was raised by the people of Acaster. To help raise funds for its construction, functions were held at the schoolroom, now School Cottage. Money was also raised by subscriptions from people who paid for a tablet of stone bearing their name. These were built into the front wall of the Hall, a large stone tablet costing £10 and a small one £5.

The Hall became a registered charity in 1963 and is managed by a committee made up of representatives of various organisations in the village. It has benefited from many improvements since first being built such as central heating, toilets and a car park, with further modernisation planned for the near future.

The names of the soldiers in whose memory it was built are recorded on a plaque on the inside of the Hall.

ACASTER ROLL OF HONOUR

Lt J E Cundall	F Forth	E Smith
G W Forth	J A S Fowler	F T Smith
Rev E R Gibbs	J O S Fowler	R A Swales
A Hudson	B Hudson	A Turner
J A Smith	F Lancaster	L Turner
G Wilkinson	S Mountain	E H Tyler
(The above were killed in action)	J D Pank	F W Tyler
H Appleton	J R Penty	J Walker
M Appleton	J A Poad	A Wood
Rev A J Crawley	A Richardson	G Wood
J H Fairburn	W Richardson	W Wragg
G Fendley	J Rushworth	A C Hudson

Figure 29 Rev Edward Gibbs.

Amongst the names of those killed is that of the Rev Edward Gibbs who, before leaving to be an army chaplain, was the Curate-in-charge of Acaster and Bishopthorpe as well as Chaplain to the then Archbishop of York, Cosmo Gordon Lang, who later became the Archbishop of Canterbury. Edward Gibbs had come to Bishopthorpe in 1913 and was made Curate-in-charge two years later, taking over from the Rev Stafford Crawley who left to be an army chaplain in France. Edward was an extremely popular figure in both parishes and was well known for his simple sermons and for transporting himself, and on occasion the Archbishop's mother, on a motorcycle and sidecar. The Archbishop and the parishioners held him in great affection, which was reflected in the large number of gifts he was showered with when he also left to be an army chaplain in the autumn of 1917. Edward Gibbs died in France on Good Friday 1918.

Another of those listed as 'Killed in Action' is J A Smith. Private John Arthur Smith of the West Yorkshire Regiment was the second son of Tom Smith, the salmon fisherman, and spent his childhood in Acaster Malbis. His two brothers, Francis Turton and Ernest Wilfred, are also listed on the Roll of Honour and their families still live in the village. Known as Jack, he married Hannah Gaines at Poppleton on 21 October 1911. They lived in Bishopthorpe and had two small children. Jack joined up in June 1916 and was killed in action on 31 July 1917, aged 28.

We feel mention should also be made of Fred Raimes' second son, Lancelot, who was killed in the

Figure 30 John Arthur Smith.

trenches in 1916. He was born in Acaster Malbis but had been ordained curate in the parish of Chipping Barnet. He joined, as a combatant, the regiment of his brother Alwyn who had been in France since the start of the war. In a letter which still survives, Alwyn heartens his brother and gives him two bits of emphatic advice: 'Make certain you have a steel helmet and keep your head down'. We do not know whether he obtained a steel helmet but we do know that he was mortally wounded by a sniper's bullet. That was within three weeks of arriving at the front and he died a day later in hospital at Bailleul. A memorial tablet was later erected in Holy Trinity church.

The only villager to fall in the Second World War was Tom Atkinson, whose parents ran the Ship Inn.

The Brickyard

Hardly would the people who broke the first turf when digging the claypit on Intake Lane have realised that they were in fact commencing what is now the centrepiece of Lakeside, the housing development completed in 1996 by Barratt (York) Ltd.

Acaster Malbis Brickworks Ltd was started in *c* 1927 by E M Dowdney (Billy) and his wife Kathleen, on land forming part of Mount Pleasant Farm. There were two other directors: Kathleen's sister, Nora Cundall and Frank Lee (Secretary). The Company's letterhead declared 'Manufacturers of facing, pressed and common bricks, tiles, etc'.

Mr Dowdney's carbon-copy book (hand written) covering the period 5 July 1930 to 16 October 1931 survives and provides both an insight into how business was conducted at that time and an interesting record of prices and labour costs. It also serves as a reminder of some of the businesses which traded at that time.

17 July 1930 Messrs The Glass Houghton & Castleford Collieries Ltd.

We thank you for yours of 16th and regret to say we cannot accept your quotation for coal as it is considerably more than we can buy at elsewhere.

17 July 1930 Messrs Allerton Main Collieries, Woodlesford, Leeds.

We thank you for yours of 16th inst and shall be pleased to accept your quotation for Washed Doubles i.e. 13/3d Thirteen shillings and three pence per ton at the Pit, and we have made arrangements for The Northern Motor Utilities Ltd York to have their lorries at your Colliery on Monday next for Twenty five tons or more. Should you require a reference our Bankers are 'The Midland Bank Ltd., Nessgate, York'.

30 July 1930 Mr. Robinson, Joiner, Holgate Road, York.

Your enquiry of this morning. We shall be pleased to accept an order from you for Twenty thousand Common Bricks price at our Yard 45/- Forty five shillings per thousand. Terms one month following delivery. As we have come down in price to meet you will you not oblige by taking say 4,000 Sand Faced Bricks at 60/- Sixty shillings per thousand. Thanking you in anticipation.

31 December 1930 Mr H Prime, Fourth Avenue, Tang Hall, York.

I have to inform you that all wages here have been reduced and we can in the event of your coming back to work only offer you 1/- One shilling per hour and work cannot be given in wet or bad weather. If you think you can do better elsewhere we shall understand. Should you resume work here, it must be clearly understood that weather permitting we must have six and a half to seven thousand bricks per day. Taking this opportunity of wishing you a Happy New Year. Yours faithfully.

One notable item of plant was Steam Fire Engine No 4850 made by Merryweather & Sons Ltd which was used to pump water; sadly, there is no record of where it came from or how much it cost.

A drying shed, 144 feet long by 30 feet wide (c 44m by 9m) and capable of holding in excess of 33,000 bricks, was erected in 1930 to enable bricks to be dried in wet weather, and in particular throughout the winter months, before being placed in the kiln (otherwise known as a clamp). The moisture content of each brick was somewhere between a half and three-quarters of a pint of water.

Villagers recall that as well as being used for brick production, a product known

Figure 31 Building a brick clamp, c 1925.

as pug was also manufactured, most probably towards the end of the brickworks' life. Pug – a sand/lime mortar mix – was used in the building industry. During the Second World War the coating of canvas sheets for the protection of damaged buildings was carried out at the brickworks, presumably utilising the large space available in the drying shed.

Bricks produced at Acaster were donated by the Brickworks for the construction of the Memorial Hall and were also used for several other properties around the village.

A deterioration in the amount of suitable clay brought about a decline in the business until it closed in 1955.

The WI and the YCA

The Acaster Malbis branch of the Women's Institute started in *c* 1930. At this time the Memorial Hall was run by a committee which was largely male and they refused to allow the women to use the Hall. Consequently, the WI met in Miss Mary Cundall's coach house at Hall Garth, christened the SS Enterprise (!), with oil stoves for heating and hot water for the tea carried over from the house.

By 1937 however the Hall was in a poor state, at which point the women were told not only to meet there, but also to run it, which they did throughout the war.

Mary Cundall was a very active president, visiting numerous other groups in spite of her lack of transport. In 1965, when Carol Woollcombe came to Acaster,

Mary relinquished the post and Carol took over. Carol was very keen on drama and under her direction the branch entered several competitions, with more than a little success. Their greatest triumph came with a Yorkshire dialect play called *Rivers of Damascus*, written by Carol herself. The set was made to look like a farmhouse kitchen and the cast consisted of Carol, Gordon Hall, Phoebe Speed, Elsie Oddy, Gwen Brown and Betty Nixon. It started rather inauspiciously with Gordon Hall, the leading man, arriving only five minutes before curtain up because he had been calving a cow! In the end however they won Best Performance, Best Set and Best Original Play – quite a triumph which caused a few ruffled feathers amongst the WI establishment! The awards were presented by Dame Anna Neagle. On that occasion the Adjudicator was a northern lady from the Lake District, which may have helped; in another year however the Adjudicator was a southern gentleman, who confessed he didn't understand a word – but he gave them the prize all the same!

In 1980 the branch celebrated its fiftieth anniversary, with two of the founder members present, Mrs Gwen Brown and Mrs Mabel Stott.

Early in 1983, because of dissatisfaction with WI HQ, moves were afoot in Yorkshire to form a breakaway movement. This was to be run on more relaxed lines but still to be rural in principle and to follow the interests of countrywomen. It was to be called the Yorkshire Countrywomen's Association. When it came to the vote, Acaster members were unanimous and in March 1983 the Acaster branch became one of the first to be formed in Yorkshire. The then president of the WI, Moira Hall, became the first chairman of the Acaster YCA. The branch is an integral part of ever-changing village life, and draws members from Copmanthorpe, Bishopthorpe and Dringhouses as well as Acaster.

Coffee Mornings and Craft Days are part and parcel of all YCA branches and from these events the Acaster branch raises creditable sums for local charities each year.

At War Again

The day war broke out we were leading corn. In those days it was all manual work, leading with horses and wagons. The corn was cut by a horse-drawn binder and the sheaves were stooked by hand and left in the fields for two or three weeks depending on the variety and the weather.

In the first few weeks of the war there was an influx of evacuees from Leeds who were placed in people's homes. After a few months when there were no air raids they went back home. We had to have the houses blacked out, no lights to be seen at night, and also the farm buildings. Soon after the outbreak of war the Local Defence Volunteers (LDV) was formed with a few local people but they had no proper rifles, only shotguns. The following year, 1940, the Home Guard was formed with Headquarters at Bishopthorpe, and they obtained a few modern weapons. The Civil Defence was formed and Captain Raimes was in charge at Acaster. We had a rota to sit up at night at the Manor and we slept on a camp bed in a small room there. When Cpt Raimes received a purple warning on the phone, this meant the German planes had just crossed the coast. If this happened during the night Cpt Raimes would wake us up and send us out on our rounds to inform the two Wardens and two First Aiders who were on duty that night that there was an air raid warning. The Wardens had to go round the village blowing a whistle to warn people that there was about to be a raid. The two First Aiders would proceed to the Institute [Memorial Hall] and stay there until the 'all clear' was announced by the ringing of a hand bell. This usually worked well except for one occasion when the man responsible for calling the Wardens and First Aiders out unfortunately returned home to bed after the all clear but did not inform them, so they were up all night! On 29 April 1942 York was bombed but at Acaster we never received a warning about this raid. A German pilot landed in the crossroads' field and was arrested by a passing policeman on a bicycle.

The War Agricultural Executive Committee was formed and officials came round the farms and ordered the farmers to plough grass out in order to grow arable crops. The land had been down to grass for a long time and was landed. I ploughed our fields with a pair of horses; it was very hard work.

(Harold Smith 1999)

In January 1940 three farms (St Andrew's, Novia Scotia and St Andrew's, Appleton Roebuck) were taken over by the Air Ministry for the construction of a grass fighter strip, a satellite of nearby Church Fenton. Recent examination of contemporary aerial photographs by English Heritage has revealed that 'field boundaries' were painted on to the ground in order to disguise the runways. Local farmers continued to use the land between the runways for food production. The site was unsuitable from the start because of its proximity to the River Ouse: the airfield was frequently non-operational due to fog.

Construction work started in the spring of 1940 and billets for the airmen and air women were erected on several farms such as Woodside, Beechlands and Nova Scotia. The joiners and building workers were taken in as lodgers by many local people. A searchlight was sited in the nineteen-acre field at Woodside Farm and remained there until the end of the hostilities.

The first aircraft to arrive at Acaster, on 6 January 1942, were the Airacobras of 601 Squadron. These American-built fighters had numerous technical problems and the Squadron lost one of their pilots when his plane crashed through ice on a flooded River Ouse. The Airacobras were soon replaced by Spitfires and in March 1942 601 Squadron moved to Lincolnshire.

The airfield was then used for training by units equipped with Oxfords. Later in 1942 the decision was made to rebuild Acaster as a bomber base. This involved the construction of concrete runways, perimeter tracks and new buildings. The airfield was never fully operational however – once completed it was used only as a relief landing ground for the Halifaxes from neighbouring bases such as Marston Moor, Riccall and Rufforth. It was also used as a bomb dump, the trees of Stub Wood providing excellent camouflage. There were numerous bomber bases around York so unfortunately the area suffered many plane crashes. On one occasion two

Halifaxes collided over Askham Bryan College, and on another a Halifax crashed into houses at the rear of the Winning Post public house on Bishopthorpe Road, killing several people.

In 1944 No.4 Aircrew School was established at the airfield. Acaster was seen as a good posting since it was only a short bus ride from York. G Sykes ran a bus service taking local people and service personnel into York daily and they prided themselves on never leaving anyone behind. The record stood at 105, with the conductor riding on the mudguard!

Part of the aircrews' training involved 'circuits and bumps' – taking off, circling round the airfield and then landing again – using the twin-engined Oxfords. One night in October 1944, after a bright sunny day, a dense fog occurred while several planes were practising night flying. About 9pm the local Civil Defence was called out to search because four planes were missing. One was found crashed in trees down the Ings road near the weir but the crew had escaped safely. Another was found on Mr Goodin's land near Stub Wood; all the crew were killed. The other two planes crashed on the far side of the river but fortunately both crews survived. Mr Ted Stott, the Air Raid Warden, received a commendation from the Civil Defence for the help given.

In the village many whist drives and dances were held during the winter to raise money for the war effort. Whist drives cost one shilling (5p) and dances ninepence; a combined ticket was one and six. Two whist drives were held specifically by the WI to raise money to send to the people from the village serving in the Forces. These raised eleven pounds and nine shillings and since there were eleven members serving at the time, they each received one pound – a large sum at

Figure 32 Airacobras lined up on Acaster Airfield, 1942.

Figure 33 Ted and Mabel Stott, Air Raid Warden and Post-Mistress, 1940.

the time. Many villagers were of course not called up because farming was a reserved occupation. After the war a committee was formed for the peace celebrations, which took place the following year.

The airfield closed in February 1946. It was then used unofficially for a variety of purposes, most notably driving lessons; there are probably several people in the village whose first experience behind the wheel was on Acaster airfield! In 1963 the airfield was sold and at one stage it was used by light aircraft from home and overseas for business and leisure purposes. This included race meetings, when owners, trainers, jockeys and even occasionally horses flew in. The Control Tower and one hanger still remain but the majority of the site has been taken over for light industrial use. The runways, meanwhile, slowly decay amongst fields of corn, a lasting reminder of the days when the roar of aircraft was a regular accompaniment to the harvest. In the early 1990s the former Sick Bay was dismantled and re-erected at the Elvington Air Museum; it is now known as the Elvington Room and is set out as the 'Briefing Room', as well as being used for functions.

Caravan Sites

Acaster Malbis is now well known for its caravan sites, which form an important part of the village's economy. The tradition of caravan sites goes back at least to the 1930s and perhaps to the turn of the century.

It is interesting to note that it was because of the caravan sites that the village was connected to the mains sewerage system in the late 1960s, which then allowed housing development to start. In 1963 the West Riding County Council approached the site owners and offered them the choice of having their licences reduced to four caravans and staying on septic tanks, or financing the installation of a mains sewerage system. Three owners, Mr C Franks (Mount Pleasant), Mr E Stott (Old Post Office) and Mr N Taylor (Ship Inn) decided to go ahead with the sewerage scheme and had to fund nearly half the cost – an immense sum. They were not very pleased when the Council announced after they had paid their final instalment that it was to connect the whole village to the scheme!

Chestnut Farm

According to one H Milward Nicholas writing in the *Yorkshire Post* of 29 May 1939, he had a friend who brought an old horse-drawn gypsy caravan to Acaster some 35 to 40 years previous. He sited the caravan on a piece of land between Garth Farm and Chestnut Farm held by Tom Smith the fisherman, which became known as 'Van Dyke Camp'. Was this the first-ever caravan park? After a number of tenants the farm was taken over in 1938 by Richard and Edith Dearlove. During their era, campers were accommodated on the paddock in front of the farmhouse, much of what is now the caravan park being a 'bog' at that time. One family from West Yorkshire who first came to the site in the 1930s have held caravans there continuously ever since – over 60 years!

In 1964 Stanley Dearlove took over from his father and proceeded to develop the farm into a caravan park. His first task was to fill in the bog with spoil (stone, bones and other remains) from the excavations at York Minster central tower restoration work! Some of the farm buildings were turned into a caravan showroom and repair workshop. In 1984 ownership transferred to his nephew Steven Smith who has further developed the park and farm buildings, as well as carrying out extensive flood prevention works – a far cry from his great-grandfather's beginnings with one caravan 100 years ago.

Mount Pleasant

The origins of the Mount Pleasant site are well documented. In about 1937 Mount Pleasant Farm was owned by Nora Cundall and her sister and brother-in-law, Mr and Mrs Dowdney. They allowed Winnie and Ralph Pollard to park their caravan three or four times a year in the field beside the farm. From the initial single caravan several more appeared, together with a number of tents.

After the end of the war in 1945 up to five families, mainly demobilised airmen and their families, took up residence and some stayed for several years. In the 1950s touring caravans became more popular and two or three came each weekend. Charges were one shilling a night (5p in today's money) or five shillings for a week. Facilities were basic to say the least: a pump in the farmyard for water and an Elsan chemical toilet (with a spade to dig a hole to bury the contents). There were no hard-standings, and electricity and piped water did not arrive until about 1960.

Both East Field and West Field were later developed to accommodate static and touring caravans, and tents. The Centre field is now a large residential site, holding some 84 Park homes.

Moor End Farm

This site is the smallest and the newest, having been opened in 1963 by G and M Hall. At that time it had just one toilet and one tap for everyone, but a new shower and toilet block was added in the 1970s to keep up with the changing requirements of campers. The holiday season was then much shorter, with campers not braving the elements until Whitsuntide rather than Easter. The campsite area was once a paddock used for raising calves and farm-bottled milk was sold at the door, visitors enjoying watching the milking and helping with the bottling. Two Dutch boys who first came to the campsite in 1966 return regularly, now bringing their wives and children with them.

Poplar Farm

One of the oldest caravan parks in the village is the Ship Inn Caravan Park. This was situated in the orchard behind the Ship Inn and is now part of Poplar Farm. Visitors came to stay in wooden chalets or brought horse-drawn caravans. Poplar Farm first opened as a campsite after the Second World War, when it belonged to Herbert Fairburn. The river frontage, known as The Green, was not originally part of the farm, being the property of Norman Taylor, one-time landlord of the Ship Inn. The riverside site was opened in 1956 and in 1968 the Taylors bought Poplar Farm and combined the two sites, Norman remaining as landlord of the Ship until 1975. The toilets and showers are housed in what was once the farm's cow shed.

The Old Post Office

The Old Post Office caravan site was initially a field used primarily by cattle and, from about 1934, the occasional Boy Scout camp. One of the stories that Mrs Stott the post-mistress used to tell was about the times when the post office had to close early; the cause – the need to repair tent damage caused by a careless cow horn. Until the early 1990s the field by the river was used for tents, with caravans on the field opposite, the former site of the windmill. The site is now run by Mrs Stott's daughter Vivienne and her husband Noel Baren.

The Slipway (The Landing)

In 1958 Mr Norman Hebden purchased the disused brickyard for the purpose of carrying out the business of boat repairer and storer. As there was no access to the River Ouse from the site, he approached the Acaster Malbis Parish Meeting to take a lease of the parcel of land known as the Landing.

It was thought at that time that the Landing had been given to the Parish by Lord Wenlock at the time of the Great Sale in 1898 but in fact it had been retained by the Wenlock family and was at that time in the ownership of the Hon Mrs Irene Constance Forbes Adam of Skipwith Hall, near Selby.

Following an approach by the Meeting it was agreed that the Landing should be conveyed to the Meeting's representative body. On 20 October 1959 the Chairman of the Meeting, Geoffrey Smith and his father took a conveyance by way of Deed of Gift of the Landing. After lengthy legal proceedings a County Court judgement in favour of the Acaster Parish Meeting was given on 14 May 1962.

The slipway was owned and run by the Members of the Parish Meeting for a short time but subsequently this was put to tender and the successful bidder was Mr F Taylor of Villa Farm.

Mr Hebden was able to operate his boatyard and used the slipway until he sold the business. The boatyard was subsequently sold and relocated to the old airfield and now operates as Waterline Leisure. Waterline also operate the slipway.

The Lakeside housing development now occupies the site of both the brickyard and the boatyard. At one time the site also housed a garage (the last source of petrol in the village) and a club ... the Playboat. The Playboat holds fond memories for many locals!

'Poach'

October 1987 brought news that shook the Acaster Malbis community to its roots; Shepherd Homes Ltd had, it was revealed, been in discussion with Selby District Council for the previous eighteen months over plans to create a new town on the disused Acaster Airfield. The news was announced by Carol Woollcombe, an Acaster Malbis parish councillor and Selby JP.

At a public meeting held in the Memorial Hall about 120 residents opposed the plan. The strength of feeling was underlined when a Copmanthorpe Parish Councillor attempted to say why he thought the proposal was a good idea. The poor individual was, according to a newspaper report 'shouted down, abused and threatened with being thrown out of the village hall' – surprisingly moderate treatment perhaps given the proximity of the Ouse!

The full extent of the plans was made known by Shepherd at another public meeting attended by more than 400 people. A complete 'village' of 4–5000 homes with a population of around 12,000 was proposed, including shops, a market, public house and other services. A new road link to the A64 would service the scheme.

The objectors vowed to fight the scheme and soon POACH (Protection of Acaster Communities and Heritage) was born, with Carol Woollcombe as Chairman and Roger Raimes as Vice-chairman and Treasurer.

'Who really pulled the plug?' – that was the question asked at a fund-raising barbecue and dance at Manor Farm organised by POACH, during which the village was blacked-out for nearly twelve hours by a power cut, due apparently to a damaged cable caused by a drainage contractor working on the airfield. Not to be outdone, the intrepid organisers called upon a local farmer from Appleton Roebuck, who loaned a generator for the barbecue lighting, the bar and of course the music.

In July 1990 Shepherd finally unveiled their scheme, named St Andrew's: cost £200 million; 2250 new homes; an area of 450 acres; population 5600; 15-acre shopping centre; public houses; churches; recreational facilities; a 30-acre nature reserve; the possibility of a new railway station on the East Coast main line with park and ride facilities into York; 50 acres for employment purposes with 2500 to 3000 jobs.

The ensuing period witnessed a great deal of wrangling involving both Selby District Council and also North Yorkshire County Council, who argued that the development was needed to protect existing communities. Final victory came in 1994 when, after a lengthy Public Inquiry, a Government Inspector's report recommended that Acaster Airfield should be included in the Green Belt.

VILLAGE CUSTOMS

Possibly the most popular village custom in the late 1800s involving the farm servants was 'ploughboying', when husbandmen from Acaster and adjacent villages gathered together as 'ploughboys' to party in and around York. The end of the holiday and celebrations was known as Plough Monday. Plough Monday was the first Monday after the feast of Epiphany (twelfth night) and marked the day when ploughing resumed. As hardly any work was done in the fields in the first days of the new year, it was a general festival: landlords feasted their tenants, the tenants feasted their servants and everybody joined in the celebrations. Initially the celebrations were confined to Acaster; servant men and labourers dressed in their best cord suits adorned themselves with ribbon knots, bows and rosettes and drew a plough through the village. Gifts of money from the villagers encouraged the participants and the local inn benefited accordingly as most of the monies raised found their way behind the bar!

In later years the show changed its character and the festivities were instead held in the city. The plough was retired and replaced by united bands made up of three to six farm workers from local villages. In terms of musical instruments, the rule was 'if you can play it, bring it', although the essential constituent was a drum, and the noisier the better!

Some groups formed themselves into a company and sent a king and queen, clowns and groups of men who took every opportunity to dance and weave intricate patterns using wooden swords.

Sadly the Plough Monday festivities have ceased, although the church continues to commemorate Plough Sunday, when a lamb and a plough are blessed.

Plough Sunday is one of the traditional country services still celebrated in the village. On Rogation Sunday, the fourth after Easter, the parishioners would perambulate the boundaries of the parish, blessing the crops. A shorter route is used today. At Lammas, the first Sunday in August, the Eucharist is made from the first-cut corn (barley these days), celebrating the importance of the new spring harvest.

Other customs were secular rather than ecclesiastical ...

A game similar to quoits is recorded as being played in the Acaster district but by the 1930s it seems to have disappeared. The brassie, surprisingly, was made of brass; it was solid and shaped like a slice of Dutch cheese. It is described as being about 90mm across and 20mm in the centre, tapering to a reasonably sharp edge. A 20mm diameter iron bar was pushed into the ground with about 150mm projecting. A sixpenny coin was balanced on the iron bar and each player took a turn in throwing the brassie at the coin and tried to knock it off the bar. If the player succeeded he then kept the coin and his opponent put another one on. The game ended when one of the players had lost half a crown.

Acaster Malbis has supported a variety of sporting organisations over the years, not least the award-winning football team of the 1920s. It is claimed that they were never beaten!

In keeping with many English villages, Acaster Malbis holds an annual Country Show, although it is a relatively modern event having been instigated by Ralph and Winnie Pollard in 1978. The Show is held in the Memorial Hall in mid August, and such is its popularity now that the recently introduced Farmers' Section has to be displayed in the car park. Entries are judged by experts from the York area and a number of trophies are awarded. The winner of the best overall entry receives the much-coveted Rose Bowl.

Figure 34 Acaster Malbis Football Team, 1923.
Back row: F Camplin; J Holmes; A Mountain; G Mountain; H Brown; E Jolley (Sec); H Foster; H Milner
Middle row: J Parker; G Forth; F Mountain; G Johnson; J Hudson; H Fairburn; Mr Heartshorn; E Wolfe
Front row: J Walker; W Littlefair; J Buckle; H Edmonds; M Appleton

11
A Time of Celebration

As a result of an open meeting held in the Memorial Hall in 1998 with the aim of establishing the interest in, and identifying means of celebrating, the Millennium an interesting array of ideas were put forward. A Millennium Committee was formed with Steven Smith as its Chairman. Volunteer groups were formed to develop those ideas which were accepted, and as each project came to fruition, it can honestly be said that Acaster Malbis did not let the Millennium go unmarked. In addition, all those who were able to contribute in any way enjoyed the experience immensely.

Fund-raising events in advance of the Millennium such as casino nights, flower-arranging demonstrations and an antiques evening were enthusiastically supported by many.

Among the events of the year were:

31 December 1999 – Millennium Eve. The lighting of a beacon (a steel basket mounted on top of an 8m telegraph pole) provided by Roger Raimes and created most enterprisingly by Andrew Dale. This was part of a nation-wide scheme which involved beacons being lit all over Great Britain, the chain progressing southwards to London where the Queen lit the final one on the Thames. About 200 people joined in the celebration in Acaster and there was a real air of fun, sentiment and expectation.

1 January 2000 was a beautiful day which saw a football match between regulars of the Ship Inn and other villagers. The teams were well supported, the spectators fortified by coffee and bacon sandwiches!

At the annual children's Christmas Party in January, souvenir mugs sponsored by the Yorkshire Countrywomen's Association were distributed to the children of the village.

On 26 March 2000, a new yew tree was planted in Holy Trinity churchyard by Carol Woollcombe, who for many years taught the Acaster Sunday School. The tree has been propagated from a yew that is 2000 years old.

28 May 2000 – Carnival Day, which included a parade of floats and a marching band. It was 23 years since the village last saw a similar event (Silver Jubilee 1977) so the organisers were determined to make this an event to remember, which it was. Children's Fun Sports, stalls, games, a flying display, teas, a barbecue and an Under 12s Disco were all arranged and the celebrations ended with a Live Jazz Evening … altogether a memorable day.

On 24 June 2000 a Grand Millennium Barbecue and Dance took place at Manor Farm ... what eaters, what dancers ...

23 July 2000 – Open Gardens Day. A rare opportunity to see ten beautiful and very different gardens around the village.

Reading this list brings a certain sense of *déjà vu*: a newspaper cutting from the *York Weekly Herald* for 1 July 1911 records the celebrations in Acaster Malbis to mark the Coronation. The children were all presented with a Coronation Mug, and the day included a cricket match, sports and games for the children, and dancing, which 'commenced at 10pm and carried on until the early hours'. In addition, Mr Raimes opened the grounds of his house, Southmoor Gardens to parishioners and provided a grand display of fireworks.

Other projects arranged as part of the Millennium celebrations include a video record of the various events, the erection of village signs at the parish boundary on all roads leading to the village and, last but not least, this book.

Figure 35 The planting of a new yew tree in Holy Trinity churchyard by Carol Woollcombe (with Rev Paul Rathbone), 26 March 2000.

Appendix 1: Tenant Lists

Hearth Tax, Lady Day 1672

Name	No. of Hearths	Name	No. of Hearths
Francis Fox	1	Ellis White	1
Willm Marfeild	1	Dorcas Marshall	1
Edwd Faucett	1	Thomas Brignall	1
Willm Ryley	2	Thomas Varley jun	2
Thomas Taylor	1	Thomas Brignall	1
John Vaux	1	John Doubty	2
Thomas Walker	1	Willm Atkinson	1
Robert Darling	1	Willm Wyrill	1
Thomas Taylor sen	1	George Dinnar	1
Thomas Dinnarr	1	Thomas Doubty	1
Ann Goodyeare	1	Thomas Varley	2
Gearge Scarborough	1	John Whitehouse	1
Thomas Tate	2	Willm Lesune	1
John Gibson	2	Edwd Vaux jun	1
Ann Trewitt	1	Ann Waid	1
William Metcalfe	1	Mathew Darlinge	1
William Woodworth	1	James Moore	2e
Thomas Teasdale	2		(meaning property empty)
William Atkinson	2	Edmd Whitehead	1
John Teasdale	1	George Waineman	collector
George Cawood	2	William Atkinson	constable
Willm Tanfield	2		

1763 Estate Map

A	John Allison	Q	George Pullen
B	Stephen Wilson	R	George Crosby
C	Samuel Hatfield	S	Mrs Hudson
D	John Fairburn	T	John Laycock
E	Elizabeth West	U	Land in Hand
F	Thomas Leedom	2.4	John Doughty – Freehold on Ingsmead
G	John Croft	•	Francis Barley Esq
H	Richard Tasker	2.9	Sir Thomas Ingleby
I	Richard Creasor	V	Thomas Chapman
K	Richard Kettlewell	W	John Doughty
L	William Emmerson	X	Elizabeth Holms
M	John Dove	Y	William Rorvel
N	Robert Stabler	Z	Robert Darling
O	Thomas Chambers	⅄	Thomas Cooper
P	Hugh Abell		

1763 Estate Map (continued)

⚴	William Stead	Δ	Thomas Edrington
2	John Martin	⳨	Robert Tanfield
3	Edward Elsworth	+	Richard Fowler
4	Matthew Beilby	Ʀ	Ann Stephenson
5	Matthew Darling	Ƴ	William Fairbourn
6	Robert Tezziman	22	William Darling
7	Thomas Stevenson	8	Robert Hubic
8	Richard Broadbelt	1	William Green
9	Joseph Fairbourn	Ƽ	William Stork
❑	Michael Darling	1.1	Matthew Beilby Freehold

1798 Land Tax Redemption

(All properties are listed as 'Farms')

Tenant	Value of Property (£-s-d)
Joseph White	£8-16-1
John Kettlewell	£16-4-11
Rebecca Cowper	£1-5-1
Philip Preston	£0-6-9
Edward Elsworth	£6-6-0
Richard Broadbelt	£1-12-6
Charles Gill	£0-6-6
Elizabeth Preston	£0-5-8
William (?) Raimes	£0-5-1
William Etherington	£15-5-8
William Cundall	£12-10-0
Philip Darling	£0-4-2
William Oates	£6-2-0
John Oates	£6-5-6
Thomas Burdon	£0-8-4
John Cooper	£0-8-4
Stephen Wilson	£0-13-6
Frances Archer	£0-9-4
Michael Darling	£1-0-10
Thomas Leetham	£0-16-8
John Cross	£1-17-6
Henry Headley	£0-3-1
John Raimes	£23-19-1
George Herbert	£5-5-8
Thomas Thompson	£15-1-0
Charles Mawson	£9-16-3
William Pickering	£12-18-7
John Milne	£4-3-10
Richard Leap	£0-5-2
William Stead	£0-3-7

York and District Directory, November 1898

Carriers to York – J H Cowper and William Buckle
Cowper, John Henry, joiner and farmer
Cowper, Robert, farmer and assistant overseer, The Hollies
Cowper, Robert, joiner, The Post Office
Cundall, Horatio F
Cundall, Robt Henry, farmer, The Poplars
Cundall, William, farmer, Mount Pleasant
Darling, Mrs Ann, shopkeeper
Dawson, John Thomas, farmer
Fairburn, George, bricklayer and Parish clerk
Gavigan, James, farmer
Holmes, Richard, flour dealer
Holmes, Henry, market gardener, carrier, and shopkeeper
Jefferson, William, steam thrashing [sic] machine owner and farmer
Poad, Robert, farmer, Broad Lane Farm
Potter, John William, farmer
Raimes, John, South Moor House
Richardson, Joseph William, blacksmith
Smith, Tom, fisherman and market gardener
Tyler, John Frederick, Ship Inn
Varley, John and Joseph, farmers, Nova Scotia
Watson, Mrs Sarah, dressmaker

Appendix 2: MSS Material

Wenlock Papers

The Wenlock Papers relating to the Escrick Park estate are held at the University of Hull Brynmor Jones Library. The Collection is large and several hundred items relate in some way to Acaster Malbis which the Thompson/Wenlock family held from 1755 to 1898. The items listed below are those that are referred to in the text.

DDFA4/1/11	11 October 1755	Bargain and Sale for £26,000 by Charles Viscount Fairfax to Dame Sarah Dawes of the manor of Acaster Malbis.
DDFA/45/4	1763	*Map of the Lordship of Acaster Malbys belonging to Lady Dawes.* Surveyed by John Stodart. Scale 20 chains to 5 ins.
DDFA/44/35	29 October 1765	Will of Sarah Thompson. Probate 14 June 1773.
DDFA4/1/16	4/5 March 1778	Lease and Release by Richard Thompson of Acaster Malbis, to Beilby Thompson of Escrick and James Hamlyn of Clovelly Court, the manor of Acaster Malbis.
	14 April 1778	Mortgage of same.
	26 May 1789	Reconveyance of same to Richard Thompson.
DDFA/32/16	17 March 1781	Bargain and Sale of 850 oak trees in Acaster Malbis.
DDFA4/1/17	16 February 1799	Redemption of Land Tax for Acaster Malbis by Richard Thompson.
DDFA/7/354	1 May 1813	Lease of land on island at Naburn Lock for the construction of a mill.
DDFA4/1/18	23 February 1820	Grant by Richard Thompson to Marie Francoise Bidgrain of annuity of £1500 charged on manor of Acaster Malbis.
DDFA/44/45	20 May 1820	Will of Richard Thompson. Probate 15 September 1820.
DDFA4/1/19	30 October 1852	Merger of Tithes in Acaster Malbis by Beilby, Lord Wenlock.
DDFA6/1	15 December 1898	Particulars of Sale of Acaster Malbis Estate.

DDFA/32/26	20 June 1899	Undertaking by Lord Wenlock to Dowager Lady Wenlock to indemnify against loss by reason of sale of Acaster Malbis Estate.
DDFA4/1/60	5 August 1899	Conveyance by Beilby Thompson to Fred Raimes of Stockton for £10,819 – Farmhouse, 2 cottages and 262.028 acres.
DDFA4/1/64	2 April 1901	Conveyance by Beilby Thompson to Fred Raimes of Stockton for £6860 – St Andrew's Farm (128.880 acres), Holly Cottage Farm (17.561 acres), Lamprey Race and Ings (.439 acres).

York City Archives

Ouse and Foss Navigation Records
M61 Grant by William Malebisse to Robert Neve of two bovates in Acaster Malbis. Ante 1176.
Hearth Tax, Lady Day 1672

York City Reference Library

An Historical Account and Pedigree of the Noble Family of the Fairfaxes with the Collateral Branches. From the earliest accounts down to the present time. Collected from the best Authorities by A Friend. Dr Burton, 1769
Robert Cooper, Map of the Ainsty, 1832
Plan of Towpaths (Y386.3)
Parish Registers
Census Returns 1991

Borthwick Institute

The Borthwick Institute has a number of documents relating to the parish, principally ecclesiastical, including a number of Terriers.
They also hold the Court Leet Manorial Records (PR AC/M8).

Miscellaneous

National Monuments Record (English Heritage)
Memorandum of Pains Laid on the 13th Day of November in the Year 1846 by the Jury of the Township of Acaster Malbis. (Private Collection)
Ings Masters Record Book (1899 to present day). Held by the current Ings Master.
Acaster Malbis Brickworks Ltd carbon-copy book. (Private Collection)

Bibliography

Appleby, K C 1993	*Britain's Rail Supercentres: York*
Baildon, W P 1907	'Acaster Malbis and the Fairfax Family', *Yorkshire Archaeol J* 19, pp 19–30
Bogg, E 1904	*Lower Wharfedale – The Old City of York and the Ainsty*
Bradley, T 1988	*Yorkshire Rivers – No 5 The Ouse* [facsimile of 1st edition published by *Yorkshire Post* 1891]
Brayley, C E W nd	*The Annals of Bishopthorpe 1215–1963*
Bromehead, J Nowill 1886	*A Sketch of the History of Acaster Malbis* (YCRL Y942.845)

Bulmer's Directory of North Yorkshire 1890

Camidge, W 1890	*From Ouse Bridge to Naburn Lock*
Cook, W J & Co 1898	*York and District Directory 1898*
Cooper, R 1832	Map of the Ainsty (YCRL)
Dobson, R B 1996	*The Jews of Medieval York and the Massacre of March 1190.* Univ of York Borthwick Paper No.45
Environment Agency	*Catch* (Spring 1999)
Farrer, W (ed) 1914–16	*Early Yorkshire Charters* 3 vols
Faull, M L and Stinson, M 1986	*Domesday Book 30, Yorkshire* (Pts 1 & 2), (Phillimore edn)
Gray, L 1996	Acaster Malbis: An Historic Site Survey (unpub dissertation, Bishop Burton College)
Knowles, D and Neville Hadcock, R 1971	*Medieval Religious Houses in England and Wales*, p 190
Lockhart, J G	*Cosmo Gordon Lang* (YCRL Y922)

OS 6" to 1 mile: Yorkshire sheet 191: 1st edition surveyed 1846, published 1851; 2nd edition revised 1906, published 1910

Ripon Historical Soc 1992	*Hearth Tax List for York City Parishes and Ainsty Wapentake*
Percy, J W (ed) 1973	*York Memorandum Book*
Smith, A H 1961	*The Place-names of the West Riding of Yorkshire* IV, pp 218–19
Taylor, J P G 1999	*Escrick A Village History*

Testamenta Eborancensia Surtees Soc 79 II, 1884, p 122

Victoria History of the County of Yorkshire: The City of York V, 1961

Victoria History of the County of Yorkshire III, 1974

Victoria History of the County of Yorkshire: East Riding III, 1976, pp 74–82

Yorkshire Archaeol J 7, 1882 'The Returns for the West Riding of the County of York of the Poll Tax laid in the second year of the Reign of King Richard the Second (AD 1379)', p 179

York Civic Records (YAJ Record Series), 5 (1946), pp 126, 132

Yorkshire Deeds (YAJ Record Series), I (1909), II (1914), IX (1948), X (1953)

Yorkshire Life, December 1968, pp 52–3